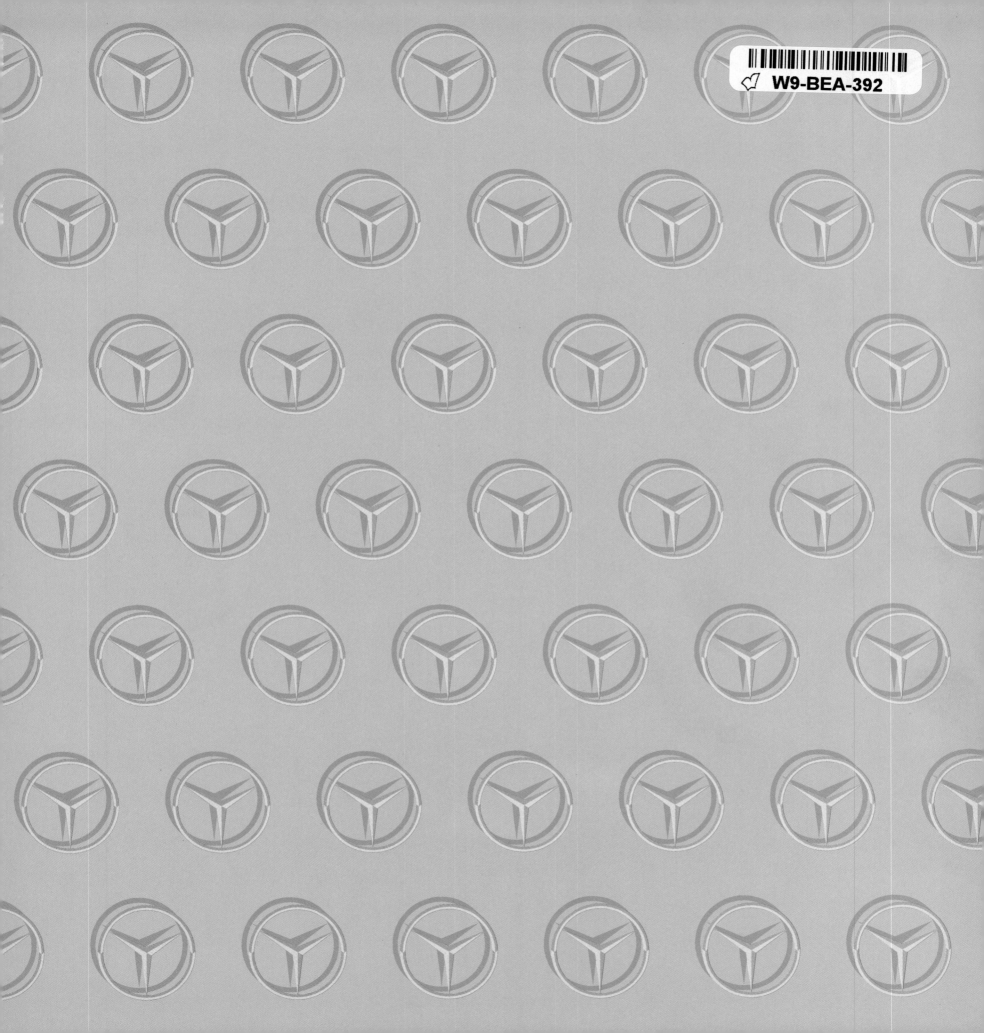

Mercedes

NOTHING BUT THE BEST

Mercedes

NOTHING BUT THE BEST

JOHN HEILIG

CHARTWELL
BOOKS, INC.

A QUINTET BOOK

Published by Chartwell Books
A Division of Book Sales, Inc.
114 Northfield Avenue
Edison, New Jersey 08837

This edition produced for sale in the U.S.A., its territories
and dependencies only.

ISBN 0-7858-0937-6

Reprinted 1999

This book was designed and produced by
Quintet Publishing Limited
6 Blundell Street
London N7 9BH

Creative Director: Richard Dewing
Designer: Rod Teasdale
Managing Editor: Diana Steedman
Editors: Keith Ryan, Andrew Wilson

Typeset in Great Britain by
Central Southern Typesetters, Eastbourne
Manufactured in Singapore by United Graphic Pte Ltd
Printed in Singapore by Star Standard Ind. (Pte) Ltd

Contents

Preface   6

Foreword   7

Introduction   8
   The Birth of the Automobile   9
   Daimler and Maybach   11
   Benz   14
   Mercedes   18

Chapter 1   20
   Daimler and Benz: Before the Merger   21
   Postwar Production   24
   Daimler and Benz Merge   26

Chapter 2   27
   First Cars from Daimler-Benz   28

Chapter 3   42
   Postwar Production Begins   43
   Safety   47

Chapter 4   48
   The 1950s   49
   The 300SL Production Car   56
   The 300SLR   62
   Mercedes Benz in the United States   64

Chapter 5   65
   The 1960s   66
   Competition   81

Chapter 6   85
   The 1970s and 1980s   86
   Birth of the C-Class   88
   Station Wagons   90
   The Fourth Generation SL   92

Chapter 7   94
   The 1990s   95
   Competition   116

Chapter 8   120
   New Directions   121
   The Future   124
   The Merger with Chrysler   126

Index   128

Preface

The first Mercedes-Benz I can remember seeing was a 300SL. I owned an MGA at the time (the early 1960s) and was entered in a gymkhana at a local shopping center parking lot. The 300SL was also entered.

I can remember looking at this strange vehicle with doors that opened up, instead of out. I knew immediately that here was something unique. Even my inexperienced knowledge of automobiles at the time told me that here was a car built by someone who wasn't using the same rules as everyone else.

The second Mercedes-Benz I remember was a 300S Cabriolet. Again, I was in the MG and was driving along. The 300S (which was the parent of the 300SL) was in another lane. When it left the road I was on, I turned to watch it go away and almost had an accident. It might have been worth it.

Since those days more than 35 years ago, I have lusted after both the 300SL and 300S, with the emphasis leaning more toward the 300S as I get older. Both are on my personal short list of the most beautiful cars ever made. Some day I would like to own one of them, although I doubt if I could afford one.

It wasn't until I began researching the history of Mercedes-Benz that I truly appreciated the heritage that goes into every automobile that comes out of the factory at Sindlefingen in Germany and now from Tuscaloosa, Alabama. There is a heritage of design and design consistency that is rare among automakers. Cadillac, for example, has used many design themes over the course of the past 35 years, but Mercedes-Benz has retained a consistency. A Mercedes-Benz from 1960 doesn't look all that different from one of 1998.

Under the skin, of course, the cars are far more sophisticated, and to Cadillac's credit, so are theirs. A Mercedes-Benz is a safe car, owing to the primitive steps taken toward occupant safety by Béla Barényi just after World War II. A Mercedes-Benz is a fast car, thanks to the efforts of some great engineers. Furthermore, a Mercedes-Benz is conservatively styled, thanks to the solid lines drawn up by the team of designers just after the war.

In writing this Mercedes-Benz history, I have been fortunate to have had the assistance of the Communications Department of Mercedes-Benz of North America under the able leadership of Steve Rossi. Steve is a knowledgeable historian himself and would have a large body of his own work if he wasn't so busy working for a living. The MBNA archives also supplied the historical photographs in this book.

Many of the original photographs were taken by my old friend Dave Gooley, a Californian who has helped me with six books to date.

It was a new friend, Quintet Publishing's Keith Ryan, however, who shepherded the manuscript and photos through to production in rapid time. It is also Keith's confidence and good humor that made my side of the bargain such a pleasure. But last, and certainly not least, I would like to thank my wife Florence and our daughters, Susan, Sharon and Laura, who are always my inspiration.

Foreword

If the dictionary definition of history is indeed "a past that is full of important events," then what better subject to include between these covers than the story of Mercedes-Benz?

The Mercedes marque is the only one that truly spans not only the entire history of the automobile, but also the phenomenal business that has matured with it as well. And rightfully so, since it was Gottlieb Daimler who first applied for patents for his high-speed, internal combustion engine in 1885, and Karl Benz who subsequently received a patent for his Motor Wagen on January 29, 1886.

As you read this book, you will quickly recognize that Daimler and Benz not only created what ultimately evolved into today's Mercedes-Benz, but they quite literally invented an industry. No doubt, Mr. Webster would certainly define that as "an important event," though it was indeed just the first of many which would ultimately turn today's three-pointed star into the crown jewel of the industry Daimler and Benz conceived more than 110 years ago.

Invention, innovation, ingenuity, intuition, intelligence, individuality, integrity – descriptors all, that would forever weave their way within the unparalleled story that is Mercedes-Benz. From research to reality, and from the test track to the race track, Mercedes-Benz has routinely set the standard for the world to follow, despite the early advertising claims from more truly parochial competitors. Then, of course, there's the legendary history of Mercedes-Benz quality, durability and reliability – a story that could surely fill a single volume in itself.

However, the dictionary also says that history is "a branch of knowledge dealing with past events," so it certainly should not be limited to only what has gone before. At Mercedes-Benz, our heritage… and thus, our accumulated knowledge… continues to fuel an unprecedented development pace that has now added an additional benefit to a product portfolio that was already second to none, that benefit being value.

No, Mercedes-Benz has certainly not stood still, and instead of a company that routinely introduced three or so new products every ten years, we have accelerated to a cycle more on the order of ten new products every three years. So, fellow automotive aficionados, you are not only reading past history, you are living in the midst of it as well.

Mercedes-Benz is simply the best. Why should any of us ever have to settle for anything less than the best, either yesterday, today or tomorrow?

We know that with our Mercedes-Benz automobiles you have never had to, nor will you ever have to settle for less; and with John Heilig's passion for putting pen to paper (or perhaps fingertips to word processor keys nowadays, though it doesn't sound quite as romantic), I know you won't have to either. You already have the best of Mercedes-Benz right in the palm of your hand.

Michael Basserman

Michael Basserman
Vice President,
Mercedes-Benz of North America

Introduction

The Birth of the Automobile

The challenge of self-propulsion had fascinated thinkers and tinkers, engineers and alchemists, for centuries. One of the earliest references to self-propulsion is in Homer's *Iliad*, where he mentions the desire to so move. Leonardo da Vinci considered ground propulsion as possible as the helicopter he also foresaw. The Dutch physicist Christian Huygens demonstrated an internal combustion engine of sorts – it used explosives to move a piston – in 1673, but the idea never progressed beyond the demonstration stage. Nicholas Cugnot developed a steam carriage in 1769, but it was used for hauling guns and not people.

Efforts were undertaken in the United States to create some form of "automobile," although it would not be named officially until the end of the nineteenth century. One early example was successful, even though it made only one run. This was the 1805 Orukter Amphibolos of Oliver Evans. Evans built this contraption under contract from the City of Philadelphia as a steam-powered dredge. After demonstrating the vehicle in the center of the city, Evans drove it to the Delaware River where it began to do the work for which it was constructed. Little thought was given to capitalizing on the land-based side of the operation.

Any success in developing a true automobile depended on the successful development of a small engine to propel it. In the Museum of Historic Vehicles, in Boyertown, Pennsylvania, there is a small spindly four-wheeler built in the 1860s by one James Hill. According to legend, Hill drove the vehicle on the streets of Boyertown in 1868, creating a racket and scaring the livestock. It was banned from ever running again and stories were allegedly written about it in the local newspaper. Unfortunately, all copies of the paper were destroyed in a fire that leveled City Hall and the exact date of the car's operation cannot be determined.

It was in Europe, though, where the development of the automobile took hold, and it was the creation of an internal-combustion engine running on a form of gasoline that gave impetus to the development.

Jean Joseph Etienne Lenoir may be credited with perfecting the gas engine. His combustion engine was patented in 1860, although it differed only slightly from horizontal steam engines of the time. As a Mercedes-Benz engineer, Fritz Nallinger, would write,

> Now, an engine finally existed which gave off no smoke, for which no firing was needed, no boiler, no heater, no fuel storage space and which could immediately be set in motion by an uncomplicated procedure. Following the exaggerated enthusiasm came the disenchantment, for all of the scientific reckoning was too optimistic. The steam engine followers noted with sarcasm that it was true that the Lenoir Engine needed no heating, but instead, it needed so much more lubrication, namely an attendant who had to oil the machine at very short intervals, otherwise it slowed down the speed and presented difficulties.

At the 1867 Paris International Exhibition, Nikolaus Otto won a gold medal for a gas engine he exhibited. Otto had begun his work in 1861, shortly after a patent was issued for what was known as the Lenoir engine. He began work on a home-made Lenoir engine. He

Above left:
Wilhelm Maybach

Above right:
Gottlieb Daimler

Right:
The first engine ever developed by Daimler and Maybach was requested by Otto in early 1875. This engine was over 12ft tall and produced only 3 horse-power.

joined forces with Eugen Langen, who was a trained engineer. In 1872, they formed a company, Gasmotorenfabrik Deutz, to build engines they developed together. By 1876, Otto was granted his own patent for a four-stroke engine.

Otto hired Gottlieb Daimler as production manager of Gasmotorenfabrik. He brought Wilhelm Maybach with him. Otto's atmospheric engines had reached the limit of their development. Power did not exceed three horsepower (hp) and the engine was more than 12 feet tall. Daimler was requested to develop a gasoline engine in early 1875. Still, Otto resumed his research and was awarded a patent in 1876 that explained the basics of the four-stroke engine.

Otto discovered that his problem was in the ignition system. He used a low-voltage magneto ignition on the fuse ignition inductors used by army engineers. We shall see how Daimler and Karl Benz worked to overcome the problems which beset Otto and managed to develop practical gasoline engines.

Daimler and Maybach

Gottlieb Daimler was an employee of Otto's, having begun working for him in 1872. He would leave in 1882 to form his own company when he realized that his goals and those of his boss were identical – Daimler just wanted to get there first.

Daimler was born on March 17, 1834, in the small German town of Schorndorf, near Stuttgart. He attended trade school and later earned a scholarship to a mechanical engineering institute. He worked for several engineering companies along the way, among them the Maschinenfabrik in Karlsruhe.

In 1863 he began employment at the Bruderhaus Reutlingen, a machine factory that employed orphans and the handicapped to teach them Christian Socialism. Daimler was appointed as supervisor. He succeeded in reorganizing the factory and was elected to the board of managers.

While he was at the Bruderhaus he met the woman who would become his wife, Emma Kurz, the daughter of a pharmacist. He also met the man who would become his partner in later years, Wilhelm Maybach, who was 12 years younger.

When Daimler was hired by Otto to become the manager of his new factory, he insisted that Maybach

Top right:
The first Daimler engine.

Right:
In 1885, Daimler installed his engine on what would be the world's first motorcycle.

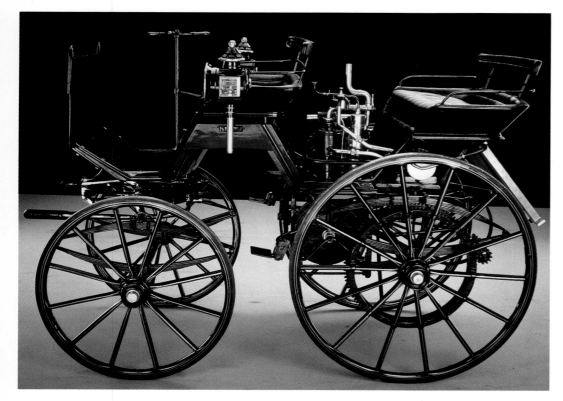

Above:
Daimler built his first "Moto Carriage" in 1886, powered by a 1.5 hp single-cylinder engine.

come along with him. When he left Otto's company, he took Maybach with him again. Daimler saw higher engine speed as the goal, and a better ignition system as a means of reaching it.

Daimler and Maybach began their own company in Bad Cannstatt, a suburb of Stuttgart. They set up a workshop in a greenhouse on the property Daimler bought. Their goal was the development of a high-speed internal-combustion engine that could power a vehicle. They realized that the limiting factor in Otto's designs had been the ignition and set about developing a new ignition system. In the space of a year they had increased the speed of the Otto four-stroke engine from 200 rpm to 600 rpm.

According to Fritz Nallinger, "The first model of the fast running, small and light gasoline engine was ready in 1883, and in its way revolutionary because of its small measurements, low weight and revolutions numbering between six hundred and nine hundred per minute as compared to one hundred to five hundred of the common five to ten times heavier stationary engine."

By August 29, 1885, Daimler had enough confidence in his new motor to submit patent specifications to the Berlin Imperial Patent Office. The drawings that accompanied the specifications showed a small one-cylinder motor on what was the world's first motorcycle, the Reitras. Daimler also installed his motor on a sleigh and a boat.

Meanwhile, Daimler ordered a small coach, an "American," from the Stuttgart coach building firm of Wimpf & Sohn. In the greenhouse, he and Maybach installed a 1.5 horsepower version of their engine on the coach. Test runs continued through the fall of 1886.

By 1888, Daimler's motor carriage was in the newspaper, where it was reported that "the experiments will now be extended to a road vehicle." By 1889, Maybach had designed a two-cylinder engine, a V2 actually, with the cylinders attached at a 17-degree angle. By this time, Karl Benz had patented his three-wheeled Patent Motor Car, and gave Daimler an idea. Maybach designed a four-wheeled carriage, the Quadricycle, that weighed only 660 pounds, and attached the motor, four-speed gearbox, rubber tires, and a steering rod. Maybach obtained some of the parts for the Quadricycle from the bicycle department of a local knitting-machine factory.

The Quadricycle was exhibited at the International Exhibition in Paris where it attracted the attention of Madame Sarazin, who would eventually provide enough business for the small company for it to continue to develop other vehicles.

Daimler's installation of his motor in a carriage was "a sincere effort to give his wife pleasure," according to Nallinger. "Then followed its installation into rail vehicles, into an air ship by Woelfert, also in a fire truck, in small vehicles, which when exhibited brought delight to the visitors to the greenhouse. Daimler was completely possessed with the idea of equipping every conceivable vehicle with his engines."

Since Daimler was confident his motors would be used in a variety of different areas, he began using as a symbol a trident, signifying the superiority of the Daimler engines on water, on land, and in the air. The trident would evolve shortly into the three-pointed star.

Kilian Steiner, who had invested in many companies in Germany at the time, became an investor in Daimler's as well, suggesting that he incorporate. Toward the end of 1890, therefore, Daimler-Motoren-Gesellschaft AG was founded. Within a matter of weeks, Daimler's backers were trying to tell him what to

do. What was worse, he was left with only 200 of the 600 company shares. Maybach never received the 30 shares promised him.

Daimler withdrew from the company, and the new company directors tried to develop their own car, unsuccessfully. They blackmailed Daimler into releasing his patents to the company or face bankruptcy. Daimler capitulated, and on October 10, 1894, signed over his patents to DMG, essentially excluding himself from

further association with the company that bore his name.

Just over a year later, however, DMG was once again foundering. New investors contracted with Daimler for him to return as general inspector of DMG. Maybach returned as technical director.

Once DMG was in the black again, the investors started another motor-car company in Berlin, using Daimler's patents without Daimler's knowledge. Daimler was also cheated out of special bonuses he had earned.

Above:
Karl Benz patented this motor car in 1886, just weeks before Gottlieb Daimler received his patent.

Benz

On the other side of town, so to speak (actually in Mannheim), Karl Benz grew up under more humble circumstances than Daimler. Karl's father, a locomotive engineer, died before he was born on November 23, 1844, in Pfaffenrot. Despite the hardship, Frau Benz worked hard to send her son to high school and to the Polytechnic College in Karlsruhe. After graduating in 1864, he began working at the Karlsruhe Maschinenfabrik. He completed his apprenticeship in three years and left for a design job at a scales factory. Gottlieb Daimler would join the Karlsruhe firm two years later.

In 1869, Benz accepted a position as a foreman in a bridge construction firm. Here he met Bertha Ringer, who would become his wife.

With an associate, August Ritter, Benz began a company to sell building supplies, but after several disagreements the two decided to part ways. In 1872, Karl and Bertha opened the Karl Benz Iron Foundry and Mechanical Workshop. Business, however, was not good, and by 1877 the wolf was at the door. He had to try a new direction. So he decided to build a two-stroke engine.

Karl had been trained in the problems of heat engines and decided to try experimenting with combustion engines. With the four-stroke engine protected by Otto's patents, Benz began working on two-stroke designs. By 1878, he had created a design that worked, albeit roughly. By New Year's Eve 1879, it ran smoothly.

Benz had no buyer for the engine, but a local photographer supplied enough money for him to continue development. In 1882, he began another company with the express purpose of developing gasoline engines. For some unexplained reason he left that company, but he soon found backers to begin yet another, Benz & Cie, Rheinische Gasmotorenfabrik, in Mannheim, on October 1, 1883. His two-stroke single-cylinder engine was developing 10 horsepower and brought income to the firm. Benz was free to develop an engine that could power a vehicle.

When Benz realized that the four-stroke design was

Right:
Karl Benz and his wife Bertha worked together in Mannheim to develop his single-cylinder engine and, later, the Benz Patent Motor Wagen.

the better technology to achieve his goal, he built one. By this time, the Otto patent on the four-stroke was declared invalid, freeing other engine builders to work on the technology. Benz's engine was a one-cylinder 954-cc unit that developed $^3/_4$ horsepower. As Fritz Nallinger wrote, though, "Benz found a way to build the engine as an organic part of the total conception of an automobile."

In 1885, Benz installed this motor in a three-wheeled vehicle. He decided on a single steered front wheel because he had not yet figured how to steer two wheels. In the summer of 1886, Benz drove this vehicle on public roads for the first time. His son Eugen had to run behind the vehicle carrying a bottle of gasoline because the vehicle had no fuel tank! The run was just over 100 yards long. But later, on July 3, 1886, the local

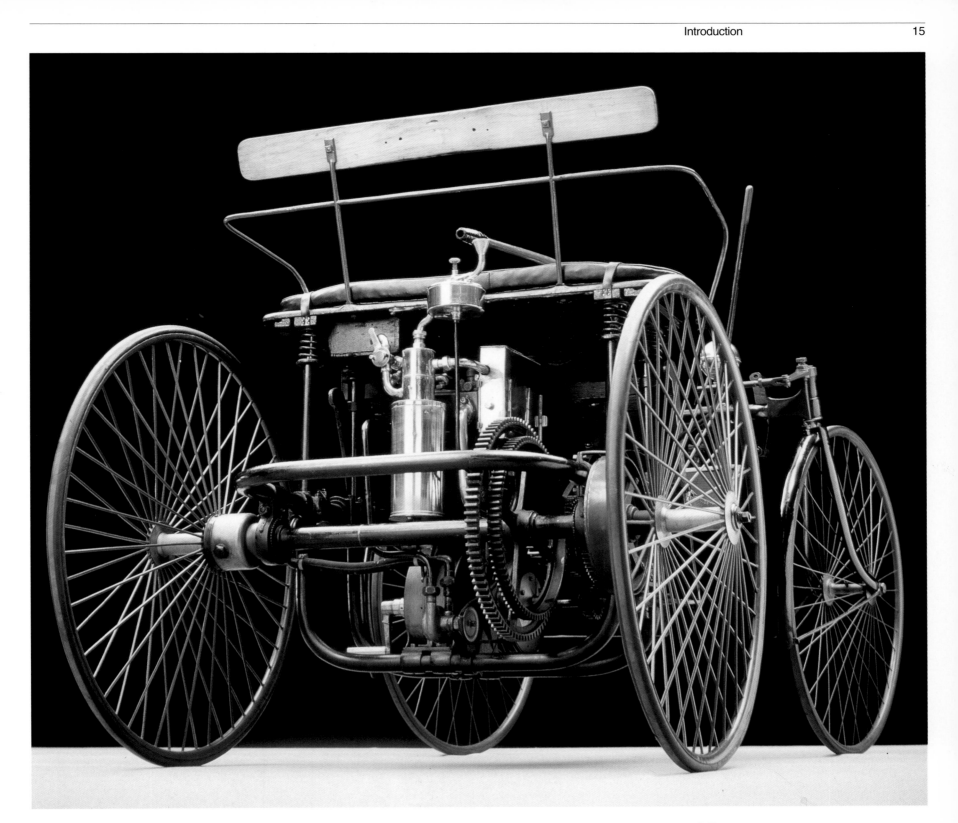

newspaper reported, "A vehicle fueled by petroleum ether which was built at the Rheinische Gasmotorenfabrik of Benz & Co. ... was today tried out on the circular road and the trial is said to have been satisfactory."

Benz built about 25 copies of his three-wheeler and showed it at the Munich Machinery Exhibition in September 1888. In November 1886, the Patent Motor Wagen earned its name when it was awarded patent number 37435. However, Benz and his partners once again disagreed on the direction the company was headed, and Benz headed off in a different direction with new partners, Friedrich von Fischer and Julius Ganss, who were interested in building motor cars.

Patent-Motorwagen ohne Halbverdeck und Spritzleder

von

BENZ & Co.

MANNHEIM.

Neue Fabrik: **Waldhofstrasse.**

Wir empfehlen ferner:

unsern **neuen liegenden** Gasmotor „Benz"
,,   ,,   ,,   Zwillingsmotor „Benz"   } mit elektrischer Zündung.
,,   ,,   ,,   Petroleummotor „Benz"
worüber auf Wunsch besondere Preislisten zu Diensten stehen.

Bertha Benz was also convinced of the efficacy of Karl's vehicles and proceeded, with their sons Eugen and Karl, to take the world's first long-distance road trip, from Mannheim to Pforzheim and back.

Eventually, Benz's one-cylinder engine would grow to 1,730 cc and 3 hp. He discovered a Munich coach builder who had a four-wheeled carriage and installed the engine in it. The car was called the Victoria, and was built from 1892 to 1900. Engines grew to 2,920 cc, always with one cylinder, and developed as much as 6hp.

Between 1894 and 1902, Benz & Cie built three production models: Velociped (or Velo), Comfortable, and Ideal. All were powered by single-cylinder motors of low horsepower. Benz wasn't concerned. His cars were selling well (1,200 Velos sold, 572 cars total in 1899 and 603 in 1900, making Benz the world's largest automobile producer), and speeds of 30 mph were adequate.

Other members of the board, however, saw a need for bigger engines, more power, and vehicles that were capable of higher speeds. They had to look no further

Above:
One of the first automobile advertisements was for the Benz Patent Motorwagen.

Right:
Karl and Bertha Benz in Benz Victoria

Below:
1893 5 hp Benz Victoria

than Stuttgart, and the successful vehicles that Daimler was building with engines as powerful as 35hp, to find suitable examples.

Julius Ganss brought a French engineer, Marius Barbarou, to Benz with five associates to design new engines. Soon, Benz & Cie had engines of up to 40 hp, including one race car.

Left:
1898 Benz Ideal

Below:
1894 Benz Velo

Mercedes

Racing was becoming important at Daimler as well. Madame Sarazin's late husband, Eduard, held the French patents on the Daimler engine. In addition to this, she had contacts with a new automobile-building company, Panhard & Levassor of Paris, which had asked for the rights to build the French Daimler engine. Madame Sarazin signed over the rights to the engine to Panhard & Levassor and Emile Levassor married the widow in 1900. Therefore, the Daimler engine was instrumental in the development of not only the Panhard & Levassor, but also the similarly engined Peugeot. Both companies went on to develop memorable early racing histories.

Above right:
Mercedes Jellinek

Right:
Emil Jellinek

In 1897, Daimler built the Phoenix, which would be the first Daimler machine to have its engine in the front. The inline two-cylinder displaced just over one liter and developed 4 hp at 700 rpm. By 1898, power had improved to 24 hp and the Austro-Hungarian Consul General in Nice, Emil Jellinek, ordered one with a shortened wheelbase to compete in the Nice Race Week events. Sadly, in this car, the company foreman and driver Wilhem Bauer was killed during a hill climb.

Jellinek ordered more race cars, but the Daimler factory was reluctant to build them, especially after Bauer's death. Jellinek persuaded the factory to build the cars by ordering a series of them and demanding exclusive sales rights for Austro-Hungary, France, Belgium, and the United States. And one other thing, he wanted to be able to sell the vehicles in his territory with his daughter's name on them – Mercedes.

Jellinek was convinced of the promotional power of motor racing. The cars he ordered had increasingly greater performance. The 1901 racer, with its 5.9-liter four-cylinder engine, developed 35 horsepower.

Besides a more powerful engine, other new ideas were incorporated on this car. For example, the intake and exhaust valves were opened and closed from below the engine by an exposed camshaft. Maybach also developed a honeycomb radiator to cool the engine. And the chassis was long and low.

Left:
The American Mercedes was the first automotive transplant, a vehicle built in a country other than its home.

Below:
William Steinway contracted with Daimler to assemble Mercedes cars in the United States.

Daimler had begun discussions with the American piano manufacturer William Steinway as early as 1888 with regard to licensing the Daimler patents in the United States. Steinway and Daimler signed an agreement whereby Steinway would build Mercedes engines in a factory in Hartford, Connecticut. When Steinway died in 1896, the company was reorganized as Daimler Manufacturing Company of Long Island City and it began building engines, launches, and a few commercial vehicles in a factory in Long Island City, New York. Steinway is said to have not seen any immediate need for Daimler's engines in automobiles, but their value to boats would be great. Nonetheless, Steinway's company did build "American Mercedes" from 1905 to 1907, when a fire destroyed the factory. The "American Mercedes" was an exact replica of the German 45-horsepower model.

Another licensing arrangement was concluded when There F.R. Simms, a director of the Cannstatt company, organized the Daimler Motor Company Ltd in England. British Daimlers were built in Coventry in the English Midlands and were the first regular production cars to be built in England. The British Daimler company became independent in the early part of the twentieth century and was later acquired by the Birmingham Small Arms group of companies. After World War II, Daimler became part of the British Leyland Corporation. William Lyons of Jaguar fame had bought Daimler, which was a neighbor on Browns Lane in Coventry. When Jaguar became a part of BMC, Daimler came along.

The British Daimler company still builds cars, although they are essentially Jaguars with fluted grilles. But the Daimler name does still live in England, although German Daimlers are no longer made.

Gottlieb Daimler died on March 6, 1900, cheated financially (in his mind) by the directors of the company that bore his name. Wilhelm Maybach continued as design engineer until 1907, when he left to form his own company. Daimler's son Paul was chief engineer from 1905 until 1923.

Jellinek's Mercedes cars were successful on the race track, as were sales of the vehicles in his territories. By 1902, Daimler, the company, recognized the truth and registered the name. As the secretary general of the Automobile Club of France said after the 1901 race season, "We have now entered the Mercedes era."

Benz also saw success on the race track, particularly in the race recognized as the first on American soil. The Chicago *Times Herald* sponsored a reliability trial on Thanksgiving Day, 1895. The winner was Oscar Mueller in a vis-à-vis Benz in eight hours and forty-four minutes.

Good news for Mercedes was bad news for Benz. After leading the world's manufacturers in 1900, Benz saw sales drop to 385 in 1901, 226 in 1902, and 172 in 1903.

Chapter 1

Daimler and Benz: Before the Merger

1914 Grand Prix Mercedes

Wheelbase (in.)	116.1
Overall length (in.)	136.0
Overall width (in.)	60.0
Overall height (in.)	40.0
Curb weight (lb.)	2376
Engine	4.5-liter I-4
Horsepower	105 @ 3100 rpm
Transmission	Four-speed

Left:
The 1914 Grand Prix Mercedes was nearly all conquering. Powered by a 4.5-liter four-cylinder engine that produced 115 hp, Ralph DePalma won the Vanderbilt Cup race in 1914 and the 1914 Indianapolis 500 in versions of the car.

The shift in racing philosophy may be seen by the results of the Semmering hill climb, contested in Austria from 1899 to 1909. Emil Jellinek won the first race in a Daimler, Ritter von Stern the second in a Daimler, and an assortment of drivers from 1901 to 1909 in Mercedes. Wilhelm Werner also was victorious in the first Mercedes outing in the 392-km (243-mile) Nice–Salon–Nice race in 1901.

Mercedes' successes were not limited to Continental Europe. Camille Jenatzy won the fourth edition of the Gordon Bennett Cup races in Ireland in a 60-hp Mercedes in 1903. A year later, William Kissam Vanderbilt Jnr set seven American speed records at Ormond-Daytona Beach in his 90-hp Mercedes. His best speed was 148.5 kph (92.1 mph). Vanderbilt was the founder of the Vanderbilt Cup races, which were originally contested over the Vanderbilt Parkway on Long Island in New York. Ralph DePalma won the 1912 and 1914 editions of that event driving a Mercedes. DePalma also won the 1915 Indianapolis 500 in a Mercedes.

DePalma's Mercedes was known as the "Grey Ghost." It was one of the 1914 Grand Prix Mercedes that had been all-conquering. The engine was a 4.5-liter single-overhead-camshaft four that was derived from an aircraft engine. It produced 115 hp. DePalma averaged 89.84 mph for his race. However, just as in 1912, the engine threw a rod through the crankcase with two laps to go. In 1912, DePalma and his riding mechanic Rupert Jeffkins pushed the car for more than a mile to the pits. They were credited with a tenth-place finish in 1912. In 1915, though, DePalma soldiered on, driving with three cylinders for the final 7.5 miles to finish less than four minutes ahead of Dario Resta in a Peugeot.

His wasn't the first Indy win for the two companies, though. Hearne was victorious in 15- and 20-minute races at the Speedway in 1910 over its new brick surface. Also in 1910, David Bruce-Brown won the first US Grand Prix in a Benz, followed by Victor Héméry in another Benz.

According to Bruno Sacco, head of Mercedes-Benz design in the 1980s and 1990s,

The Mercedes grand prix car of 1914 (built by Daimler) was not only highly successful, its design features represented a new step forward and set trends for the design of future sports-oriented cars up to the end of the 1920s. The wedge shape, although it is more easily identifiable in outline than in the vertical profile; the smooth sides, the front axle mounted well forward, and the long hood: all these features distinguish this pioneering effort.

Benz's renaissance began in 1903 with the arrival of engineer Hans Nibel. His first efforts were directed at improving the performance of the Parsifal. By 1904, engine output had improved from 18 hp to 80 hp. Nibel also eliminated the antiquated two-cylinder engines that Benz had been using in favor of four-cylinder. Engines were cast in pairs, with two camshafts and side valves in a T-head.

Along with better performance by their road cars came an emphasis on competition. Where there was a 60-hp racer in 1903, there was a 120-hp model in 1908. The first true Benz race car was a 1908 with a massive 15-liter four-cylinder engine that produced 158 horsepower. All had chain drive because the prevailing philosophy was that shafts weren't able to withstand the engine's torque.

Chassis for Benz cars of the era consisted of channel-section side members, semi-elliptic springs for the front and rear suspensions, and artillery-style wooden wheels.

One of the more significant Benz cars of the era was the Blitzen Benz (or Lightning Benz, but this is a term that is better left untranslated). This 200-hp chain-drive racer evolved from a 1908 race car built for the Prince Heinrich Trials. It used a 12.5-liter four-cylinder engine. Benz built three of these cars.

The predecessor of the Blitzen set a new distance record in a 426-mile race from St Petersburg to Moscow. While 426 miles constitutes a good day's driving on today's modern highways, in 1908 it was completed without benefit of paved roads, or roads of any kind in most cases. Bruno Sacco, in his treatise on the design of Mercedes, Benz, and Mercedes-Benz cars, had this to say about the design of the Blitzen Benz: "The form of this vehicle is marked by the special consideration given to aerodynamics as a design element. The characteristic beak shape at the front, which was conceived as a purely functional feature, will be seen again in later vehicles, and not just those of Benz."

Perhaps the Blitzen Benz's greatest successes came at the hands of cigar-chomping Barney Oldfield. Oldfield has been described as the most famous American driver of all time. Bernd Eli Oldfield was born in Ohio in 1878 and earned his first prizes in bicycle racing. He was in Salt Lake City when he heard that Henry Ford was building a pair of race cars. He headed east and bought one of the nonworking cars from Ford. He tinkered with it, painted it red, and put "999" on the side, naming it after a New York Central railroad train. With this car Oldfield set the American mile record at 55.8 seconds in 1903.

Driving a 150-hp Benz, Oldfield set a world speed record of 83.8 mph for the standing start at the 1909 Indianapolis 500. When he drove a Blitzen, he hit 131.7 mph in the flying mile and 88.8 mph for the standing mile on the hard sands of Ormond-Daytona Beach, Florida. After that, Oldfield took the car on a barnstorming tour of the United States, putting on shows and setting new speed records at tracks all across the country.

A former Buick race driver, Bob Burman, took a 1911 version of the Blitzen Benz on another barnstorming tour. He began by heading to Daytona and breaking Oldfield's speed record, taking just 25 seconds to cover the mile for a speed of 141.7 mph. It was a record that would stand for 13 years.

While the chain-drive Blitzen was setting records, Benz shifted to shaft drive in 1910 for its road-going cars. Benz built a variety of four-cylinder models, from a tiny 18-hp version with a 1,950-cc engine to a 100-hp version with a massive 10-liter four. Benz built its first six-cylinder car in 1914, the 50-hp 21/50 with a 5.3-liter engine.

According to the historian Richard Langworth, in *Mercedes-Benz: The First Hundred Years*, "It was at about this time that Karl Benz drifted away from his company (he was well into his 60s by now) and moved to building Sohne-Benz models at a factory in Ladenburg. However, the cars produced by the original Benz firm continued to be built at Mannheim."

Right:
The 1909 Blitzen Benz was one of the first racers to exhibit attention to aerodynamics. In the Blitzen, Barney Oldfield set a world speed record for the flying mile at Daytona Beach, Florida, and barnstormed around the country.

1909 Blitzen Benz

Wheelbase (in.)	109.1
Overall length (in.)	120.0 (est)
Overall width (in.)	52.0 (est)
Overall height (in.)	45.0 (est)
Curb weight (lb.)	3335
Engine	21.5-liter I-4
Horsepower	200 @ 1600 rpm
Transmission	Four-speed
Fuel tank (gal.)	72 liters

Postwar Production

A fter World War I, Benz built only eight new models, but three of these were significant. The 1921 Type 260 used a 2.6-liter inline four, but it was the first Benz model in which all four cylinders were cast *en bloc*, or together. The 2.6-liter engine was rated at 30 hp at 2,000 rpm. It used a Zenith carburetor and had a chain-driven side camshaft.

In 1923, Benz built four examples of the Tropfenwagen, a 2.0-liter rear-engined six rated at 80 hp. This teardrop-shaped open-wheeled car was entered at Monza in 1923. The Tropfenwagen used an engine with two overhead camshafts. A street version with headlights and wing-type fenders was built, but it never went into production.

Finally, in 1923 came the 16/50 sport, with a 4,160-cc six in which the cylinders were cast in threes. This was considered one of the fastest Benz production cars with a top speed of almost 70 mph.

Daimler/Mercedes did not focus entirely on competition in the first quarter of the twentieth century,

although the company's vehicles were successful at venues in Europe and the United States. Then, as now, racing provided a means of experimentation, development, and testing of new models and ideas.

One of the new ideas was a Knight sleeve-valve engine. Paul Daimler first heard of the sleeve-valve technology in 1908. Its inventor was an American, Charles Y. Knight. The essence of the Knight engine was the increased improvement in speed and performance through the high-speed introduction of air and gasoline into the combustion with the associated high-speed discharge of the exhaust gases. This was achieved through the elimination of normal intake and exhaust valves, replaced by slide valves to open and close the intake and exhaust ducts. These sleeve valves slid up and down between the piston and the cylinder wall.

With this technology, the power-to-weight ratio of the engine was improved and they were more efficient as well as quieter. However, it soon became evident that lubricating the valves would be a problem.

Below:
The 630K, with a supercharged 6.3-liter inline six-cylinder engine, was the first Mercedes-Benz designed by Ferdinand Porsche. The original car had a 12-foot wheelbase, but the "K" version used a shorter one.

Left:
Ferdinand Porsche joined Daimler in Austria, where he designed the Prince Heinrich model. He joined the parent company in 1923, and would go on to develop the Volkswagen in the 1930s and Porsche sports car in the 1950s.

Daimler achieved the patent rights to the Knight engine in 1910 and applied the use of the technology in engines for limousines and ambulances. Mercedes installed a Mercedes-Knight engine in the Daimler Krankenwagen (ambulance) of 1913, for example, which sold in the United Kingdom. Another model using the engine was the 2.7-liter 10/30 with a limousine body. The Kaiser was driven in a 16/40 with a 4.0-liter four-cylinder engine.

These engines weren't strictly for the road. Leon Elskamp piloted a 45-hp Mercedes-Knight to victory in the 1913 Belgian Automobile Club Grand Prix at an average speed of just under 100 kph (62 mph) for 381.6 kilometers (237 miles).

Daimler/Mercedes contributed to Germany's war efforts during World War I. Daimler supplied its DF80 aircraft engine, which was a development of the six-cylinder 28/95 that went on sale shortly before the war began. While Germany was in ruins after the war, the engineers at Daimler Motoren Gesellschaft made use of the experience they had gained in supercharging engines for aero applications. Supercharging was a relatively simple method of boosting the power of a small engine. After the war, Mercedes engineers applied supercharging to automobile engines.

The first Mercedes car to use a supercharger was the 1922 10/40/65 two-seater. The designation represents the German taxable horsepower, 10; the power output of the engine without supercharger, 40; and the output with the blower engaged, 65. Daimler used two-blade Roots superchargers, vertically mounted at the front of the engine and driven through small clutches and gearing off the crankshaft. When the driver wanted more power he would put the accelerator pedal to the floor, engaging the clutch and putting the supercharger into play.

Supercharged engines were the last major contribution to Mercedes engineering by Paul Daimler, Gottlieb's son. His successor was a 48-year-old Austrian, Dr Ferdinand Porsche, whose first car for Mercedes-Benz was the Type 630, with a 24/100/140 6,240-cc supercharged inline six. Porsche's original interest was electricity and he designed vehicles for the Viennese Lohmer company with electric motors at all four wheels. Porsche joined Daimler in Austria in 1905, where he was responsible for the Prince Heinrich model, which dominated racing in 1910. When Austro-Daimler split from the parent company, Porsche designed several small six-cylinder cars for the independent firm. He left when the company chose not to produce a 2.0-liter engine he had designed.

In 1923, Porsche joined DMG in Stuttgart as technical director, replacing Paul Daimler. His first efforts in Stuttgart were directed toward a series of large supercharged engines. His 2.0-supercharged eight-cylinder car was a class winner in 1924 races.

Road cars were based on this racer with long wheelbases of 12 feet and more, pressed-steel frames, I-beam front axles and live rear axles with semi-elliptic springs. The engines in the road cars were a 15/70/100 4.0-liter six and a 24/100/140 6.25-liter six. The Roots superchargers were installed at the front of the block and forced pressurized air into the carburetor where the fuel was added.

Daimler and Benz Merge

Encouraged by the success of their aircraft engines, in 1915 Daimler decided to buy a piece of land in Sindlefingen on which they wanted to build aircraft. However, after their defeat in World War I, German aircraft production was prohibited. Not only that, inflation tore into savings and the political climate was unstable, cutting into car production. The plant in Sindlefingen eventually became the body works for Mercedes and is the main production facility at the end of the twentieth century.

Under these conditions, negotiations between Benz and Daimler began, but with no outcome. It was still too soon to consider a merger.

Benz was managed more conservatively, but its problems were found in the person of the stock market speculator Jakob Schapiro, who bought large numbers of cars, paid for them on credit, then held them without paying for them until they were worth little, thanks to rampant inflation. In 1921, for example, he purchased 200 Benz chassis in this manner. He soon acquired 40 percent of the shares of the company. In July 1923 he was on the supervisory board and a year later could say he owned 60 percent of the shares of Benz, 25 percent of Daimler. Schapiro also owned Dixi and Cyklon, NSU, NAG, and Hans-Lloyd.

With inflation working in his favor, Schapiro moved funds from one company to the other and borrowed money from one company to buy others. When the economy began to stabilize, however, Schapiro's empire began to shake.

In the early 1920s, Wilhelm Kissel, who was a director of Benz, saw that Schapiro could bring Benz into bankruptcy and looked for a partner to help out the speculator from the auto company. Negotiations with Daimler were resumed. In May 1924 a contractual and sales association between Daimler and Benz was set up. A joint subscription was negotiated to even the balance sheets, with Daimler allocated 65.4 percent and Benz 34.6 percent.

In June 1925, Kissel found himself appointed to the board of both Benz and Daimler. It was his responsibility to prepare for the merger, which would take effect on July 1, 1926. The merger actually became effective on October 17, 1926.

The eminent Mercedes-Benz historian Jürgen Lewandowski writes,

> Schapiro was initially enthusiastic about the merger since he thought that he could now also have a hand in determining the fate of Daimler. Wilhelm Kissel, however, had taken precautions. With Dr Emil Georg von Strauss, the representative of the board of the Deutsche Bank, he resolved to block Schapiro's attempts to gain even more influence. Schapiro tried, when he felt resistance to his plans, to place a pistol at the head of the firm of Benz by canceling all orders – and was then most astonished when Kissel readily accepted all cancellations.

Eventually Schapiro's stake in the joint company fell to just 16 percent. After the bank took over Dixi and BMW in 1929, he left the supervisory board of Daimler-Benz AG.

Despite the fact that the Daimler people didn't particularly like being led by a Benz man, Kissel worked hard and successfully for Daimler-Benz. Together with the engineer Friedrich Nallinger and chief designer Hans Nibel, who had also joined DBAG from Benz, Kissel took control quickly. He remained chairman of the board until his death in 1942. He achieved this remarkable feat by recognizing where the strengths of the company were. By 1927, Benz models had all but disappeared from the common range of models except for light commercial vehicles.

One of Kissel's first acts was to initiate a comprehensive review of the finances of the joint firm. Prior to the merger, each factory and plant had its own accounting department and could work with the banks individually. Kissel introduced centralized bookkeeping in Untertürkheim and joined sales, advertising, and public relations at the main factory.

In 1927, final assembly of the cars was shifted to Untertürkheim, with bodies built at Sindlefingen. In October 1929, the board decided to shift production completely from Mannheim to Untertürkheim. By 1930, production had been completely shifted.

Chapter 2

First Cars from Daimler-Benz

Previous page:
The 1926 Type 600 was powered by a supercharged 6.0-liter inline eight-cylinder engine. Its styling would mimic the quintessential Mercedes-Benz prewar lines of long hood and short trunk with a tall, chromed honeycomb grille.

Below:
While it wasn't a style leader, the 1926 Mercedes-Benz Stuttgart was one of the first cars introduced by the merged companies. With an assortment of engines of various sizes, the Stuttgart would appeal to a wide variety of customers.

After the merger of 1926, Daimler-Benz introduced several significant automobiles that proved the worth of the union. The first two paid homage to the homes of the two founding companies, namely Stuttgart and Mannheim.

The Stuttgart was powered by a 2.0-liter six-cylinder engine that developed 38 horsepower. More than 10,500 of these models were sold, making it the bestselling Daimler-Benz model of the 1920s. More important, though, the six-cylinder engine was the basis for the following 2.6- , 2.7- , 2.9- , 3.2- , and 3.4-liter engines. All used the same 100-mm stroke, but varied the bore.

1928 Stuttgart

Wheelbase (in.)	110.6
Overall length (in.)	159.8
Overall width (in.)	66.1
Overall height (in.)	70.9
Curb weight (lb.)	2530
Engine	2.0-liter I-6
Horsepower	38 @ 3400 rpm
Transmission	Three-speed
Top speed	44 mph

Above:
Prince Heinrich outside the Mannheim factory, behind the wheel of a 300 Mannheim model Mercedes, 1926, with (l. to r.) Messrs Nibel, Walb and Pflanz standing by.

In 1926, Mercedes-Benz introduced the 300K, with a six-cylinder, 3.0-liter engine that developed 55 horsepower. Ferdinand Porsche was the chief engineer at the time and had intended for the car to be powered by an eight-cylinder 3.0-liter supercharged engine. The governing board of the company thought that engine was too expensive and opted for the less expensive six-cylinder model. A year later, the 300K had a slightly larger 3,030-cc engine that still developed 55 hp. It, in turn, was replaced by the 320 Mannheim in 1928 with a 3,131-cc engine that developed 58 horsepower. Acceleration improved with the larger engine and a better rear-axle ratio. Eventually, the Mannheim models grew to 3.5-liter capacity and 70 hp. The last model in the series, the 350 Mannheim, was developed after Porsche had left Mercedes-Benz. Its design was finished by Hans Nibel.

By the time the Stuttgart and Mannheim series had reached the end of production, Karl Benz would be dead. The man who invented the Patent Motor Car and loaned his name to one of the two founding firms of the great worldwide automotive industry died in 1929 at the age of 85. He had the opportunity to see the fruits of his efforts, while Gottlieb Daimer, who died 29 years earlier, missed out on any opportunity to see how *his* work would endure.

Following the Stuttgart and Mannheim models was the supercharged 620, introduced in 1927. This model would go on to be one of the most successful Mercedes-Benz production cars in competition. The 620 used a Porsche-designed 6.25-liter engine that was rated at a modest 110 horsepower in normally aspirated form. But when the Roots supercharger was bolted on, power increased almost 50 percent to 160 hp.

The 620 was followed by the 630, with a slightly larger engine, and then the 630K (K for "kurtz" or "short"), with a wheelbase 150 mm (5.9 inches) shorter than the original. Overall length of the K cars was a mere 192.9 inches on a wheelbase that stretched 133.9 inches. This is the *short-wheelbase* version. For comparison, a modern S-Class Mercedes is 205.2 inches long on a 123.6-inch wheelbase.

Right:
The 630 was based on the Model K. Its 6.3-liter supercharged engine was rated at 140-hp, five more than the K. The 630 was only available in a long wheelbase version with four bodies, including this coupe.

Below:
The 630K, with its 6.2-liter supercharged inline six-cylinder engine, had classic 1930s styling; spare tires mounted on the fenders, running boards, and rear-hinged doors.

Successive short-wheelbase versions included the 680K, with a supercharged engine that developed 270 hp, and the 680S, with two spark plugs per cylinder.

Dr Ferdinand Porsche was instrumental in the development of the experimental 700SS (SS for "Super Sport"), which evolved into the competition version, the 710SS of 1929–30. For competition, Mercedes-Benz

630K	
Wheelbase (in.)	133.9
Overall length (in.)	186.4
Overall width (in.)	69.3
Overall height (in.)	72.8
Curb weight (lb.)	4400
Engine	6.2-liter supercharged I-6
Horsepower	160 @ 3100 rpm
Transmission	Four-speed
Top speed	89 mph

drilled the chassis to make it 250 lb lighter and created the 720SSKL (L for "Leicht" or "light"). Porsche left Mercedes-Benz in October 1928 just after the SSK was introduced, after a particularly argumentative meeting of the Daimler-Benz board of directors. He was replaced by Nibel, who had come over from Benz.

The SSK used an overhead-cam, six-cylinder engine that put its power to the wheels through a four-speed-transmission, torque-tube driveshaft and rear axle.

The blower was bolted to the front of the engine and forced air into the carburetor through a long finned tube that ran alongside the left side of the engine.

720SSKL

Wheelbase (in.)	116.1
Overall length (in.)	167.3
Overall width (in.)	66.9
Overall height (in.)	49.2
Curb weight (lb.)	2974
Engine	7.1-liter supercharged I-6
Horsepower	300
Transmission	Four-speed
Top speed	143 mph

Above:
The 1928 720 SSK was the last Mercedes-Benz to show the influence of Ferdinand Porsche. "SS" stood for Super Sport. The SSK was supercharged ("K" stood for Kompressor). The racing version was the 730SSKL ("L" for Leight or light), with a drilled chassis that was 250 pounds lighter than standard.

The engines had a cast-iron cross-flow cylinder head and a block constructed of Silumin, an aluminum–silicon alloy. Inlet ports were on the left and exhaust ports on the right. Pairs of ports were joined to three flexible pipes that exited through the hood and down to the exhaust system under the car. It is these exposed exhaust pipes that define the SSK cars. As Karl Ludvigsen wrote in *Car Collector*, "These were not the first cars to have such an exposed exhaust, but they were certainly the first to give it such visual impact on a roadgoing car and also the first to impress on the public mind an association between these exposed pipes and a supercharged engine that was exploited so well later by Auburn, Cord and Duesenberg."

Again Karl Ludvigsen:

The SSK … was strictly limited to two passengers with its shorter wheelbase of 116.1 inches. Yet it did not have the high hood line, as the "SS" part of its name suggested. Instead it was low-built in just the same manner as the Model S. This combination of a long, low hood with an extremely short passenger compartment gave the SSK the most stunning proportions of all the cars in this six-cylinder series. It also made the cockpit so exceedingly cramped that it was most unusual for the chassis to be fitted with closed touring bodywork like that on the Corsica cabriolet. Most were bodied as open roadsters. As such, they exerted a riveting attraction and were indisputably the most imposing and covetable road sports cars of their era. They were also fast, with a top speed in excess of 110 mph in standard form.

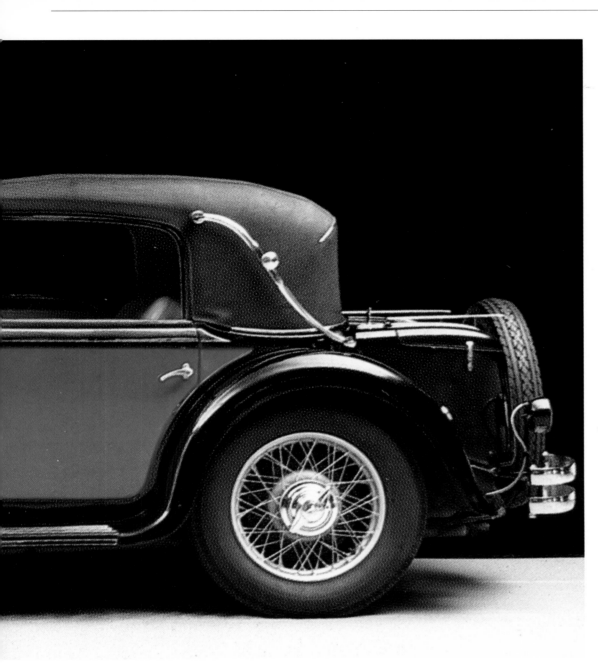

370S Mannheim	
Wheelbase (in.)	112.2
Overall length (in.)	176.4
Overall width (in.)	68.1
Overall height (in.)	58.3
Curb weight (lb.)	3410
Engine	3.7-liter I-6
Horsepower	78 @ 3200 rpm
Transmission	Three-speed
Top speed	73 mph

Above:
The 1931 370S Mannheim Cabriolet was the first car to show the design influence of Hans Nibel. The two-seater had a 3.7-liter inline six-cylinder engine rated at 78 hp.

At the same time it was developing the K series, Mercedes-Benz was working on the S (sports). This group of cars was developed primarily for competition, but they could be bought by private customers, either for racing or as the basis for a swift custom-bodied car.

The first of these models was the 370S Mannheim, with a 180-hp 3.7-liter engine. The car was developed by Nibel, who had come to the joint Daimler-Benz from Benz. This car had a shorter wheelbase than the 370, by 5.9 inches, and an engine that developed 78 hp, three more than the 370. It was available only as a two-seater and became the dream car of the 1930s.

Derivations of the 370S were the 370K, which was actually longer than the 370S, and the experimental 370K Mannheim II, which was built to test a new two-joint, swing-axle rear suspension.

Continuing the sporting tradition of the S series and the K series was the 500, introduced in 1933 with a 5.0-liter inline eight-cylinder engine rated at 100 hp. The 500K offered a supercharger that boosted power output to 160 hp, and the 540K used a 5.4-liter supercharged eight-cylinder engine rated at 180 hp with blower. Performance of the 500K was stirring for its time: 0–62 mph in 16.5 seconds, 0–80 mph in 30.5 seconds. Top speed was a mild 85 mph unsupercharged, but one could get the 500K up to 102 mph with the blower engaged.

Suspension was independent at all four corners, using coil springs. The suspension was designed by Fritz Nallinger, who would go on to become chief engineer at Mercedes after World War II and would, with Rudolf Uhlenhaut, begin the renaissance at Mercedes.

Ludvigsen writes that these were very good performance figures *for their day.* "Cars that could authentically top 100 mph, as standard production models, were still rare in the 1930s."

The larger engine of the 500K was necessary because of the great chassis weight. A 500K tested by *The Motor* in 1936 had a total weight of 5,430 pounds on a 3,418-pound chassis, for example.

These cars were the German Duesenbergs. The chassis were outstanding and the often-custom bodywork was exquisite. Mercedes-Benz often designed factory bodies for these cars that were the equal of the

Left:
With a 5.0-liter supercharged inline six-cylinder engine, the 500K offered power and the first example of classic 1920s Mercedes "style."

Below:
The 500K was not all performance. The rear compartment gave passengers exceptional comfort.

Below right:
Even though the 500K was a car that was built by the joined companies, the grille of the car was decidedly that of the pre-merger Mercedes.

Bottom:
Drivers of the 500K operated a large thin steering wheel that was much in the style of cars of the era. What they felt was what made the difference.

500K

Wheelbase (in.)	144.5
Overall length (in.)	222.4
Overall width (in.)	70.2
Overall height (in.)	65.0
Curb weight (lb.)	5236
Engine	5.0-liter supercharged I-8
Horsepower	160 @ 3400 rpm
Transmission	Four-speed
Top speed	98 mph

Above:
The ultimate 540K was the Special Roadster, originally designed to honor the 50th anniversary of the Benz Patentmotorwagen.

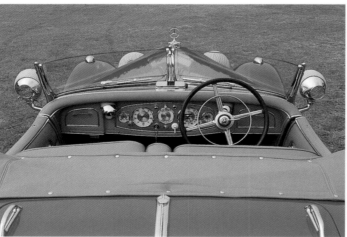

Right and far right:
This is the view seen by drivers of the 540K, including several members of Hitler's Third Reich. Gustav Röhr was director of passenger car development for Mercedes and was responsible for the 540K.

custom houses. The ultimate 540K was the Special Roadster, built for the Berlin Auto Show to honor the 50th anniversary of the Benz Patentmotorwagen. This was the most expensive Mercedes-Benz car up to that time. It was painted silver and had leather upholstery and a mother-of-pearl inlaid dash.

The 540K was the work of Gustav Röhr, who became director of passenger-car development after Nibel died in October 1934. Röhr died less than three years later, when passenger-car development was

assumed by Max Sailer and Max Wagner.

Only 400 of these magnificent cars were built. Naturally, they attracted the attention of the members of the ruling Third Reich, and several of Hitler's cabinet members drove, or rode in, 540K cars.

Car Collector magazine, in a 1983 poll among its readers, selected the 1935–39 Mercedes-Benz 500K/540K roadsters as the Most Beautiful Car, ahead of the 1936–37 Cord 810/812 convertibles and the 1930–36 Duesenberg J/SJ phaetons.

540K

Wheelbase (in.)	144.5
Overall length (in.)	222.4
Overall width (in.)	70.2
Overall height (in.)	65.0
Curb weight (lb.)	5720
Engine	5.4-liter supercharged I-8
Horsepower	180 @ 3400 rpm
Transmission	Four-speed
Top speed	104 mph

The "Grosser" Mercedes

Another model that attracted attention from political and military leaders was the "Grosser Mercedes," or large Mercedes. First introduced in 1930, the Grosser Mercedes had a 7.7-liter engine rated at 150 hp without supercharger, but a supercharger could be installed. With blower power increased to 200 hp. It was the prestige car of its day.

One particular Grosser Mercedes was built for Kaiser Wilhelm II, with the three-pointed star replaced by the imperial coat of arms. The Kaiserwagen was modified in 1941 so that it could carry the Kaiser's coffin after he died.

A later version of the 770 Grosser Mercedes was built toward the end of the 1930s and into the 1940s. Like its predecessor, it became a favored car of the new

Below:
Perhaps the ultimate Mercedes-Benz K car was the 1936 540K, with a 5.4-liter supercharged straight eight engine that was rated at 180 hp. A special silver-painted version, so attired to honor the 50th anniversary of the Benz Patent Motorwagen, was the highlight of the 1936 Berlin Auto Show.

Above:

With a 1.7-liter inline four-cylinder engine, the 1937 170V was the forerunner of many economical Mercedes-Benz models that would see the company through World War II. Versions of this car were the first cars produced by Mercedes-Benz after the war.

"royalty," the Third Reich. With supercharger, the latter Grosser Mercedes was rated at 400 hp, but it was all needed to move a vehicle that could have weighed as much as five tons.

Besides the luxury cars, Mercedes-Benz also built a series of economy and experimental cars with some novel drivetrain configurations. The 130 of 1933–36 used a 1.3-liter inline four of 26 hp. It was the first rear-engined car built by Mercedes-Benz. During testing, the 130 was equipped with a conventional grille to disguise its true engine location. In production, the nose of the car was rounded, not unlike the Chrysler Airflow but more attractive. A jeep-type variation was also built for the government.

On the 150 of 1934, which was designed to be a sports sedan, the engine was moved from its location behind the rear axle in the 130 to just forward of it. Only five of these cars were built, with their aerodynamic fastback body style. Still, it was capable of speeds approaching 75 mph.

Next in line among rear-engined cars was the 160, with a body that resembled the postwar Renault sedan. With a 38-hp engine, this model received decent sales success, with almost 1,000 produced.

The 160V, however, was a front-engined car with a frame built up of oval tubes. Considered to be Hans Nibel's most important design, the 160V and later 170V became the base Mercedes-Benz models up to the 1950s and were the cars that helped the company recover from World War II. Among the more attractive

170V	
Wheelbase (in.)	112.0
Overall length (in.)	168.1
Overall width (in.)	61.8
Overall height (in.)	61.4
Curb weight (lb.)	2420
Engine	1.7-liter I-4
Horsepower	38 @ 3400 rpm
Transmission	Four-speed
Top speed	66 mph

body designs was a two-seater convertible that had an air of sportiness about it, albeit with a traditional Mercedes-Benz grille.

During World War II, Mercedes-Benz built versions of the 170V that would run on producer gas (a combination of carbon monoxide, hydrogen, and nitrogen) and charcoal. Military versions were also built, often with their engines located in the rear of the vehicle to improve traction.

In July 1936, the National Automobile Industry Association placed orders with Daimler-Benz and Dr Porsche GmbH for 30 Volkswagens apiece. Mercedes-Benz built the cars to Porsche's designs with a 24-hp, 986-cc, air-cooled engine located behind the rear axle. Since it was a Porsche design, it is difficult to credit the car to Mercedes, but the company did build it and it was the prototype for the beloved Beetle.

Bruno Sacco calls the "pseudo-aerodynamic" Volkswagen "cuddly," and says its eventual success was more a result of this feature than its harmony of design. "It is a kind of flattering neuter which is accepted because, fundamentally, it says little," wrote Sacco in *Mercedes-Benz Design*. "A truly bad manifestation of the spirit of the age."

Mercedes-Benz also built an experimental front-wheel-drive car, the 130V, from 1936 to 1938. The car was designed by Gustav Röhr, and used a 1,277-cc flat four-cylinder engine rated at 32 hp. The four-door body had doors that were hinged at the A and C pillars. There was no central B pillar, so entry and exit were easier. Röhr died in 1938 and further development of the cars ended at that time.

Daimler-Benz's competition cars achieved worldwide success in the 1930s. The Silver Arrows, as they all became known generally, were essentially unstoppable. Only Alfa Romeo from Italy, with the great Tazio Nuvolari driving, and the German Auto Union were able to challenge the racers from Stuttgart.

The success began with the W25, introduced in 1934. Powered by a 3,360-cc supercharged inline six-cylinder engine that produced 354 hp, the W25 won its first time out. Manfred von Brauchitsch drove it to win the Eifel race at the Nürburgring.

The car was built to conform to the newly-introduced international 750-kg formula that dictated the maximum permissible weight of the racer including

W25

Wheelbase (in.)	107.3
Overall length (in.)	111.0 (est)
Overall width (in.)	64.0 (est)
Overall height (in.)	40.0 (est)
Curb weight (lb.)	1650
Engine	3.5-liter supercharged I-6
Horsepower	354 @ 5800
Transmission	Four-speed
Top speed	192 mph

Below:
This 1937 Mercedes-Benz W125 Grand Prix car was the offspring of the W25, which dominated the 750 kg formula then in force for Grand Prix racing. With a 3.5-liter supercharged engine, the W25 won its first time out, in the Eiffel race at the Nürburgring.

wheels, but not fuel, coolant, lubricants, or tires. The W25 was designed by Rudolf Uhlenhaut and the team managed by Albert Neubauer.

The racers were originally painted a brilliant white. But when they reached the race track and were weighed, they came up 2 kg (nearly 4½ lb) over the allowed maximum. Neubauer decided to strip the paint, leaving the bare aluminum body. The cars made the weight and earned forever the nickname "Silver Arrows." All Mercedes racers up to the cancellation of racing in 1955 thus were painted silver. Modern racers, which must pay homage to various sponsors, no longer carry the legendary colors.

At the end of the season, a W25 with an aerodynamic body was fitted with one of the 3,990-cc, eight-cylinder engines planned for the 1935 season. With two Roots superchargers and a double overhead camshaft head that allowed four valves per cylinder, the "B" engine produced 430 hp with the right gasoline. Rudolf Caracciola achieved 316.38 kph (196.16 mph) with the car.

The successor to the W25 was the W125, arguably the most powerful prewar racing car. With a 5.7-liter, supercharged, inline, eight-cylinder engine producing as much as 592 hp, the new car was to dominate the final year of the 750-kg formula. Rudi Caracciola won the German, Swiss, Italian, and Czech grands prix as well as the European and German championships, repeating his sweep of 1935.

The 750-kg formula was becoming dangerous. Mercedes-Benz had developed a 650-hp, six-liter

engine that propelled a speed-record car to a top speed of 437 kph (271 mph). So a new formula was instituted. It called for a maximum displacement of 3.0 liters supercharged and 4.5 liters unsupercharged. Mercedes-Benz produced a V12 engine, which was rated at 468 hp. In the W154, Caracciola won the European championship for the third time, taking the French, Italian, and Swiss grands prix. In a specially bodied aerodynamic W154, he set two new world records – the standing mile (204.5 kph/126.8 mph) and the standing kilometer (177 kph/109.7 mph) in February 1939. During the 1939 racing season, Caracciola won the German road-racing championship and the German Grand Prix. Hermann Lang won the European driving championship in a sister W154.

W154

Wheelbase (in.)	107.5
Overall length (in.)	167.3
Overall width (in.)	68.9
Overall height (in.)	39.8
Curb weight (lb.)	1870
Engine	2.9-liter double supercharged V-12
Horsepower	468 @ 7800 rpm
Transmission	Five-speed
Top speed	201 mph

Chapter 3

Postwar Production Begins

Stuttgart was a favorite target for Allied bombers during World War II, and the Mercedes-Benz factory was prime among those in the industrial city. Therefore, Mercedes-Benz had a lot of rebuilding to do if it was to return to automobile production.

The attacks against Mercedes and Stuttgart were well founded. As Beverly Rae Kimes wrote in *The Star and the Laurel*,

> Daimler-Benz products were as much a part of the German war effort as GM, Ford and Chrysler products were of the American or Rolls-Royce aircraft engines were of the British. From a German standpoint Daimler-Benz's leading contribution was probably the development and production of the DB600 series aircraft engines, those V12, fuel-injected, turbocharged power plants that were in practically every important Luftwaffe plane, not the least the Messerschmitt 109. In addition there was the normal complement of trucks, tanks, and whatever else it took to move a modern army. The aircraft engine program had begun in the mid-1930s when Fritz Nallinger left the vehicle group and took over what was euphemistically called "large-engine" development. That Nallinger and his people did their job well is a matter of history.

Despite the devastation, despite the loss of morale from a lost war effort, more than 1,200 Daimler-Benz workers were at Untertürkheim less than two weeks after the end of the war in Europe. With picks, shovels, and bare hands they began cleaning up the factory. After they cleaned the surface rubble they discovered that the machinery was relatively intact.

The first projects for the Mercedes-Benz workers were the repairs of trucks for the American Army. Wilhelm Haspel was removed as head of the factory until he was "de-Nazified" by January 1, 1948, although he continued to run the company quite effectively from his home. Otto Hoppe was installed in his place by the military government.

Plants were closed during the winter of 1945 because of the shortages of coal and electricity. Haspel's number-one goal was to rebuild production facilities and return the company to producing automobiles. Permission to build new vehicles was granted in the spring of 1946 and Mercedes-Benz, like auto

manufacturers all around the world, began by building a prewar vehicle, the 170V. Only 214 vehicles were built in 1946, most with flatbeds or boxes at the rear to convert them for use as trucks. In 1947, 1,045 were built and some were passenger cars.

That postwar 170V differed only slightly from the prewar version. Powered by a 1.7-liter four-cylinder engine rated at 38 (later 45) horsepower, the 170V was simple, but it served a purpose. Whereas it was offered with rear-engine, in two-seater sports roadster and producer-gas-powered versions in the 1930s and through the war, the postwar car was more conservative and intended to serve two purposes: provide transportation for the German people and restore some semblance of manufacturing at both Daimler-Benz and in Germany.

The 170V had an X-frame chassis constructed of oval tubes, with a wheelbase of 112 inches and an overall length of 168.7 inches. It had a top speed of approximately 65 mph and used four hydraulically operated drum brakes to stop.

In May 1949, Mercedes brought out the 170D, with a 1.7-liter diesel engine of 38 hp powering the 170. The car was identical to the 170V except for the engine. Production increased from the 214 units of 1946 to 1,045 in 1947, 5,116 in 1948, 17,417 in 1949 and 33,906 in 1950. Mercedes-Benz had returned to life.

Also in 1949, Mercedes introduced the 170S, with a body that would predict what the future 300 series would look like, but now with a 52-horsepower 1,797-cc engine. The 170S was a two-seater convertible with rear-hinged doors, sweeping fenders, and a honeycomb Mercedes grille that was tilted rearward slightly for aerodynamic effect. The canvas top had S-shaped "landau irons" that evoked an earlier age. It had a maximum speed of nearly 75 mph.

The larger engine of the 170S was used in sedans as well. The 170 continued in production until 1955.

Mercedes' first postwar six-cylinder car was the 220, introduced in April 1951. The 2,195-cc engine was rated at 80 hp and could propel the 220 to a top speed of 140 kph (87 mph). The 220 was offered in a full style

1951 220

Wheelbase (in.)	112.0
Overall length (in.)	177.4
Overall width (in.)	66.3
Overall height (in.)	63.4
Curb weight (lb.)	2970
Engine	2.2-liter I-6
Horsepower	80 @ 4600 rpm
Transmission	Four-speed
Top speed	85 mph

Above:
The 220 Cabriolet, introduced in 1951, was Mercedes-Benz's first postwar six-cylinder car. The inline six delivered only 80-hp, but it would be the forerunner of later, more powerful cars.

Right:
Inside the 220 Cabriolet, leather upholstery interior and easy-chair comfort greeted the passengers. Wood trim added a touch of luxury to the car.

range of sedan, coupe, two-seater convertible and four-seater convertible. More than 18,000 were produced in the three years of the model's life.

The Mercedes 300 series

The most significant early postwar model was the six-cylinder 300, introduced in November 1951 and built until March 1962. With exquisite styling, it was hard to believe that the 300 came from a company that was in ruins less than seven years earlier. It was offered in sedan, coupe, four-door convertible, and landaulet forms. The 300S was the sport version of the 300 series and, with a 175-horsepower version of the 2,996-cc engine, provided the power plant for the dominant 300SL coupes and sports racers of the mid-1950s.

Above:
The 300 may well have been Mercedes-Benz's most significant postwar model. The styling, both inside and out, echoed prewar cars, but the 3.0-liter six-cylinder engine would be the powerplant of one of the most dominant race cars in history.

Left:
One could easily mistake the postwar 300 for a prewar car. With a long hood, and headlights mounted on a bar connecting the fenders, it held definite 1930s highlights. But underneath, it was a modern automobile.

Above:
The 300 from the rear looks like a prewar car, since the headlights integrated into the front fenders are less obvious.

The 300 and 220 series were the first postwar Mercedes cars to use styling that integrated the headlights into the front fenders. Therefore, Mercedes concentrated on designing a rear suspension that could accommodate variations in load and still maintain full comfort and road holding. Thus was born the swing-axle/coil-spring rear suspension that was introduced on the 170V and combined with hydraulic shock absorbers.

In base form, however, the 2,996-cc engine was rated at 115 hp with one overhead camshaft in an aluminum head and two Solex downdraft carburetors. It used a cast-iron block with removable plates so that the water jackets could be inspected before final assembly. Power reached the wheels through a four-speed manual transmission with the shift on the steering column. John Dugdale wrote that the German manufacturers, like the British, could not afford to develop automatic transmissions on a par with American gearboxes. The 300 was built on a 120-inch wheelbase and was 194.9 inches long. Top speed was 96 mph.

300	
Wheelbase (in.)	120.1
Overall length (in.)	194.9
Overall width (in.)	72.4
Overall height (in.)	63.0
Curb weight (lb.)	3916
Engine	3.0-liter I-6
Horsepower	115 @ 4600 rpm
Transmission	Four-speed
Top speed	95 mph

The 300 also incorporated hydraulic steering dampening. A telescopic shock absorber was mounted between the frame and the middle section of the three-piece steering linkage. It absorbed road shocks that would normally be transmitted through the steering linkage to the steering wheel and to the driver.

Safety

Modern Mercedes-Benz is justifiably proud of its accomplishments in the field of automobile safety, both for the occupants of its vehicles and for the people who might encounter Mercedes-Benz vehicles in accidents. In early 1998, for example, when there was a great hue and cry in the United States about the disadvantages small-car occupants might have in an accident with a sport utility vehicle, Mercedes pointed out that the bumper height of its ML320 was in line with that of its C-Class sedans and would not override the sedan's bumpers in a head-on or rear-end accident.

While Mercedes proudly promoted that its stable bodywork would enable passengers to exit one of its vehicles even if the vehicle overturned, the true beginning of Mercedes-Benz's intense safety research began in 1939 when Béla Barényi joined the company. Barényi interviewed with Wilhelm Haspel and Karl Wilfert. Wilfert had known about Barényi and some of the work the young man had published, including an article that appeared in the American *Automotive Industries*.

Barényi was deeply interested in passive automotive safety, that branch of auto engineering where the car is least apt to injure its occupants. Barényi was given a 9x12 wooden hut in which to work.

Reduced to sweeping streets after the war, Barényi was rescued by a former employer, Marcel Corneillat. His wife gained employment as a cordon-bleu chef. In 1948 he was permitted to rejoin Mercedes-Benz along with Dr Haspel, who had hired him in 1939.

Barényi had designed a car of the future, the Terracruiser, with seating for six, a central driver position, a "cradle bearing" elastic suspension for the passenger cell, rear-mounted engine, and aerodynamic bodywork. A later design, the Concadoro, was a study for a "proper Volkswagen." It, too, had cell-type construction to protect the occupants.

Barényi was also responsible for the design of a car in 1925–26 that he called "The Volkswagen to Come." This car used an aerodynamically contoured body on a platform frame with a steering box mounted behind the front axle for safety. The engine was mounted behind the rear axle with the transmission mounted ahead of the axle.

In two books published in 1951, Barényi felt he was libeled with regard to who was the real inventor of the Volkswagen, Ferdinand Porsche or Béla Barényi. In a 1954 ruling, Barényi was judged to be the true inventor of the Volkswagen and not Porsche.

While his designs for new vehicles were interesting, Barényi's work on production vehicles began with the W120 series, which included the 180 and 220 sedans. These vehicles served as the model for him to use to transform his ideas into production. His main work dealt with modifications to the framework and the application of light metals in combination with synthetic resins. The 1959 220 was the first vehicle with bodywork focused on safety. This car had a rigid passenger cell and impact-absorbing zones.

Mercedes-Benz's first crash tests were conducted in 1959 in Sindlefingen. The results of these tests were that occupants in a 50-kph (32-mph) head-on crash had very little chance of survival. Doors would tend to fly open and one-quarter of the fatalities would be caused by the occupants' ejection from the vehicle. As a consequence, Karl Wilfert patented the wedge-form door lock, which prevents doors from opening of their own accord following an accident.

Safety belts, seat mounts, steering-wheel design, and design of the dash were all investigated in sled-run-staged accidents. Dummies were used to simulate occupants of vehicles and a wooden ball was used to test interior fittings.

From these early beginnings under Barényi's direction, the Mercedes-Benz safety department grew. Mercedes now investigates every accident involving a Mercedes-Benz car in Europe to determine, as much as possible, the causes of the accident, occupant injuries, and vehicle condition. The company has the most extensive database of accident statistics in the world, which is used to aid in the development of future safety in Mercedes-Benz automobiles.

Ironically, Mercedes-Benz was not allowed to investigate the accident involving Britain's Princess Diana, in which she was killed in an accident involving a Mercedes-Benz S-Class sedan in France in August 1997.

Chapter 4

The 1950s

Pontons

In 1953, Mercedes-Benz introduced a model that, in different guises, would last nine years. It was made with four different engines and sold more than 890,000 examples. This was a car with a rounded body that was affectionately called "Ponton" or "Pontoon."

Introduced in 1953 as the 180, with a 1.8-liter four-cylinder engine rated at 52 hp, it employed a new chassis design that incorporated high sectional steel side members joined to the floor of the body to create a rigid platform that resisted twisting. Mercedes-Benz claimed the platform was twice as rigid as the former X-shaped oval-tube frame, and reduced noise. The engine and front suspension were carried on a sub-frame that was attached to the front of the platform on rubber mounting blocks. In the rear was a double-joint swing axle, carried over from the previous sedans.

The 180 had a top speed of 78 mph. In June 1957, Mercedes replaced the 1,767-cc engine with an 1,897-cc unit rated at 65 hp. In 1961, a further variation of the car was introduced with larger brakes, a wider radiator, and no vertical bumper guards.

Bruno Sacco, who headed the Mercedes-Benz design department in the 1980s and 1990s, said, "The W120 (the 180 of 1953) is seen today (1988) as the object which proves that even then there was an in-house design philosophy in existence, even if we didn't like to declare it publicly. Compared to a few of its contemporaries, the W120 was very restrained and conservative. Compared to its predecessor, the 1949 170/220, it symbolizes an enormous step forward in the design field. The W120 can be seen as paving the way for the next decisive step in design."

Four months after the gasoline-engine version, Mercedes-Benz introduced the 180D, with a 40-hp, four-cylinder, diesel engine. This would be Mercedes-Benz's most successful model to date, with more than 118,000 examples sold. It employed the same frame-platform as the gasoline version, as well as the body. The only difference was the addition of a "D" to the model badging.

With the 1,897-cc engine, the Ponton became known as the 190. The engine was a detuned version of the 190SL power plant, developing 84 horsepower on a 7.5:1 compression ratio. With the compression ratio increased to 8.5:1, the engine's output reached 90 hp. Top speed approached 90 mph.

In April 1961, Mercedes-Benz began building the "C" version of the 190, with a new body. No longer rounded, the new 190 was far more angular and even had tail fins, short and curving outward slightly at the top. The engine was the same 1.9-liter four. This body was shared by the diesel-engined version and was the same as the 220 of the same era.

However, *this* finned 220 was itself a derivation of an earlier 220 in Mercedes-Benz's product explosion of the early 1950s. Born at the 1956 Frankfurt Auto Show, the 219 was the second model introduced at that show. The 219's body was similar to the 190, qualifying it as a Ponton, but had a wheelbase that was 3.9 inches longer. With a 2,195-cc six-cylinder engine that was the same as that in the 220 sedan, it developed 92 horsepower, later 100 hp, with a compression ratio increase from 7.6 to 8.7:1.

Also introduced at Frankfurt in 1956 was the 220S, with the same body style as the 219 and the same engine, but tuned to 112 hp, later 124. Considered a sportier version of the Pontons, the 220S was also available as a convertible or coupe. While these did not offer the power of the 300 series coupes and

Left:
The 220S/SE Cabriolet, introduced in 1956, was one of a class of cars called "pontons," or pontoons, giving recognition to the rounded fenders and overall styling of the cars. The classic "Mercedes grille" is obvious from this angle.

1956 220S	
Wheelbase (in.)	111.0
Overall length (in.)	185.6
Overall width (in.)	68.5
Overall height (in.)	61.0
Curb weight (lb.)	2915
Engine	2.2-liter I-6
Horsepower	100 @ 4800 rpm
Transmission	Four-speed

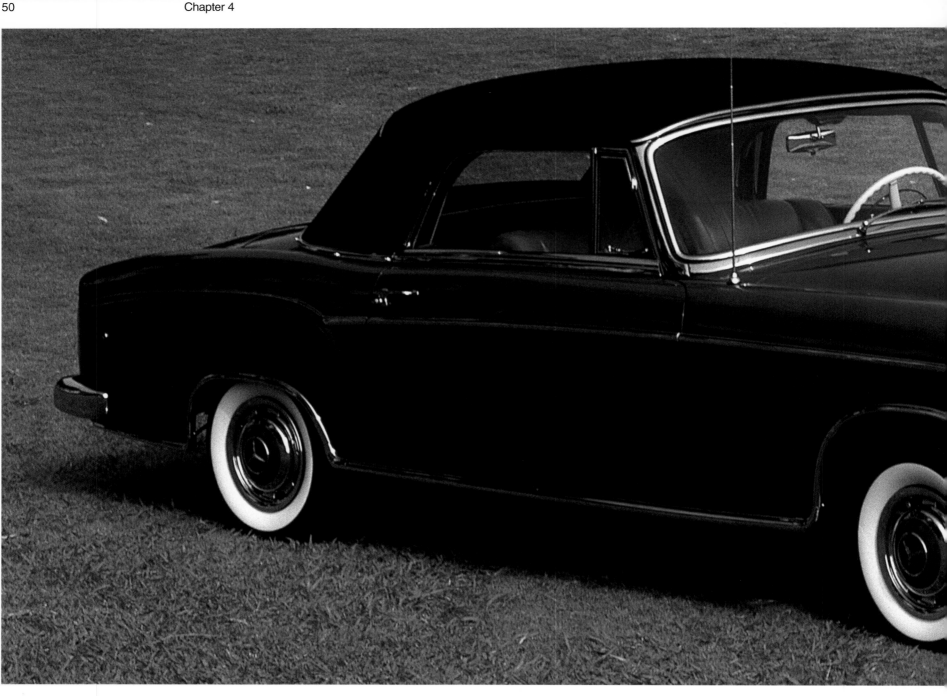

convertibles, they did show that the appearance of a rather pedestrian sedan can be improved by removing the two rear doors.

The ultimate expression of the Pontons was the 220SE – "S" for Super, "E" for Einspritz or fuel-injected. Replacing the twin Solex downdraft carburetors was a Bosch two-plunger manifold fuel-injection unit that succeeded in improving horsepower from 112 (SAE) to 134, and top speed to a tick under 100 mph. Despite an estimated additional cost of $400 for the injection system, it added 18 percent more horsepower, 5 percent more torque, and reduced fuel

consumption by a dramatic 8 percent.

Two-door convertible and coupe variations were also offered, and actually remained in production a year longer than the sedan. Total production of the 220SE was not great by Mercedes-Benz standards, about 4,000 total cars, split evenly between the sedan and coupe/convertible. But the model served to introduce relatively high-volume fuel injection to production cars.

Production had returned to respectable levels by the early 1950s. It was time for Mercedes-Benz to once again bring the Silver Arrows to glory on the racing circuits of the world. They were surprisingly well

Above:
With fuel injection replacing the twin Solex carburetors, the 220SE developed 134-hp, compared to 112 for the base 220. The extra power boosted the top speed to 100 mph.

win the 1951 German Grand Prix in a normally aspirated 4.5-liter Ferrari, Neubauer reasoned that development of the W165 would only create a car that would be on a par with the competition, not better. Mercedes decided to build a new car.

For 1954, the Grand Prix limits would be 750 cc for supercharged cars and 2,500 cc for normally aspirated cars. Mercedes-Benz decided instead to build a sports car to conform to the 3.0-liter limit for that class.

Neubauer related his thoughts in his autobiography, *Speed Was My Life*:

> We needed at least a year to design and build a new car. It would not be ready before 1953. To spend millions of marks on a racing model that would last only one season was obviously out of the question. And yet to put our racing plans on ice until 1954 was also a depressing thought. I suddenly decided to go to Paris and try to have the formula [1.5 liters for cars with superchargers, 4.5 liters without] extended until 1954.
>
> I employed all my not inconsiderable powers of persuasion, and finally succeeded, after a great deal of lobbying, in gaining admission to the decisive meeting of the Commission Sportive Internationale [CSI].
>
> After pleading that Mercedes' re-entry into international motor racing would give it a new fillip, I failed… But our chief designer, Dr [Fritz] Nallinger, came unexpectedly to the rescue. "How would it be if we developed a sports model out of our latest private car, the 300? We might then consider…" He left the sentence unfinished, but I knew perfectly well what was in his mind: sports car racing.
>
> The head of our research department, [Rudolph] Uhlenhaut, was just as enthusiastic as I was. For whole days and nights he brooded over blueprints and finally produced something completely new: an extremely light tubular space frame. The only difficulty was the doors. How were they to be built in?
>
> Nallinger and Uhlenhaut found a novel solution: the driver entered by way of upward-opening gullwing doors.
>
> I'm never likely to forget May 2, 1952, the day my second youth began, the day Mercedes-Benz returned to motor racing for the first time since 1939.

prepared. Albert Neubauer, the organizational genius who had directed the Mercedes team in its 1930s battles with Auto Union and Alfa Romeo, was still around. So was one of the W165 racers, which had been spirited into Switzerland by Rudi Caracciola before the war and was owned by the Swiss Mercedes-Benz distributor.

But where to compete? What venue would be best to display the abilities of Mercedes-Benz? Neubauer considered a development of the W165 with the postwar Grand Prix engine limit of 1.5 liters for supercharged cars. However, after seeing Albert Ascari

The car Mercedes-Benz created used a triangulated steel space frame that weighed a mere 110 pounds. The lattice of small-diameter tubes was similar to that used by Jaguar in its C-Class racer and in the Aston Martin DB2. With the tubing running high along the sides of

the car for structural stability, an unusually high sill was created. A coupe body style had been chosen and normal doors were out of the question. The solution was to hinge the doors at the center of the roof and have them open upward. When both doors were open the car resembled a bird in flight – gull wings.

In the first car shown to the press, the doors extended only to just below the window frame. In the later cars that were used for competition, they extended about halfway down the side. Eventual production cars that were developed out of the racing models had doors that reached about two-thirds of the way down the side.

Still, with the wide sill and high stepover height, entering the car was a challenge.

What the designers never considered was how the driver would exit from the car if it happened to turn over and was lying on its roof. Fortunately, the situation never occurred.

For an engine, Mercedes engineers chose the 3.0-liter six-cylinder power plant from the 300S sports coupe. In the 300 sedan, introduced in 1951, the six-cylinder 3.0-liter power plant used a single overhead camshaft, cast-iron block and aluminum head. It used two Solex downdraft carburetors and, with a 6.4:1 compression ratio, developed 115 horsepower. In the 300S sports coupe, Mercedes-Benz increased the

300S Sport Coupe

Wheelbase (in.)	114.2
Overall length (in.)	185.0
Overall width (in.)	73.2
Overall height (in.)	59.4
Curb weight (lb.)	3872
Engine	3.0-liter I-6
Horsepower	150 @ 5000 rpm
Transmission	Four-speed
Top speed	107 mph

compression ratio to 7.5:1 and added a carburetor, increasing output to 147 horsepower. For the racer, the compression ratio was increased to 8.0:1. Three carburetors, two fuel pumps, a modified camshaft that changed valve opening times, lightweight pistons, and a modified cylinder head produced 175 horsepower.

Mercedes-Benz named the racer using the company's standard nomenclature procedure, engine capacity divided by ten with letters further defining the model. Thus, the 300SL, as it was named, meant it had a three-liter engine. The S meant Sport and the L, Leicht, or light.

Below:
While the top was not removable, as in the Cabriolet, the 300S Coupe was a slightly more civilized, if less dashing, version of the 300 class. The four-door sedan was even more conservative.

The coupe body of the 300SL was extremely aerodynamic, with an estimated coefficient of drag (Cd) of 0.25. As a comparison, the best modern cars have Cd ratios of approximately 0.30. Karl Wilfet in Sindlefingen is credited with the design of this seminal car.

Mercedes-Benz entered the 300SL in the 1952 Mille Miglia. Three cars were entered, driven by Karl Kling and Hans Klenk, Hermann Lang and Erwin Gruppe, and Rudi Caracciola and Herr Kurrle. Lang crashed shortly after the start, but Kling led at the halfway point. He was later passed by Giovanni Bracco in a Ferrari 250S. Bracco won by four and a half minutes. It would be the only defeat for the 300SL.

In the next race, a sports-car-supporting race before the Swiss Grand Prix, the red-, white-, and blue-painted cars placed first and second. Caracciola had been in fourth place when he crashed into a tree, breaking his leg. He later retired.

At LeMans in June, four cars were entered. Three ran, with the win going to Lang and Fritz Reiss, followed by Theo Helfrich and Norbert Niedermeyer in second place. Kling and Klenk retired.

Hermann Lang won the next race, a sports-car-supporting race prior to the German Grand Prix at the Nürburgring. In the last race of the season, the Carrera Panamericana in Mexico, Kling was the overall winner. An American driver, John Fitch, was disqualified for backing over the starting line on one stage, but continued regardless of this and set the fastest time on the final leg.

The 300SL was retired after its nearly perfect initial season. Mercedes-Benz decided to concentrate on Grand Prix racing for 1954. The company would then return to sports car racing in 1955 with the eight-cylinder 300SLR.

Right:

With its removable hardtop in place, the 300SL Roadster resembled the earlier Coupe, but it had "normal" doors and a more unified headlamp assembly. From the numbers on the hood, it is evident that the Roadster developed a competition heritage.

Below:

With a better space frame design, the 300SL Roadster was able to be built with "normal" doors, rather than the gullwing doors of the Coupe.

300SL Coupe	
Wheelbase (in.)	94.5
Overall length (in.)	178.0
Overall width (in.)	70.5
Overall height (in.)	51.2
Curb weight (lb.)	2882
Engine	3.0-liter I-6
Horsepower	215 hp
Transmission	Four-speed
Top speed	159 mph

The 300SL Production Car

Above:
With its doors opened, it is easy to see how the 300SL Coupe earned the appelation Gullwing Coupe.

Right:
Driving the 300SL Coupe could be likened to sitting in a sauna. Ventilation was not ideal for the six-cylinder engine, and engine heat found its way into the passenger compartment.

When the 300SL became a production car in 1954, the austere racer gained a few refinements that made it an outstanding model. First, Mercedes-Benz added direct fuel injection, which increased horsepower to 219. As in the racer, the engine was tilted 45 degrees to the left side to create room for it under the low hood. On the production car, two "power bulges" added strength to the hood and gave a sense of power.

Top speed increased to 162 mph with a 3.25:1 rear end. Power-assisted drum brakes were on all four wheels. The suspension was the same as on the racer: independent in front by unequal-length double wishbones, coil springs, and telescopic shock absorbers, a swing axle in the rear with the rear half-shafts located by coil springs and telescopic shocks, mounted behind the axles rather than in front as on the sedans.

Besides the power bulges on the hood, the designers added "eyebrows" over the wheel arches that reduced the purity of the slab-sided racer, but looked much better. And since there had been a problem with engine heat making the interior of the racers exceedingly warm, exhaust vents were cut into the front fenders and fitted with 4x3 grilles to reduce discomfort to the driver and passenger.

"The now legendary 300SL Gullwing of 1954 can be classified as a virtuoso performance in a sy mphony of design," wrote Bruno Sacco in *Mercedes-Benz Design*. "The design and styling concept have a racing pedigree, and are only slightly 'civilized.' The true designers of the 300SL are to be found among the engineers who, in 1952, were able to put a successful racing car on the circuit."

Entering and exiting the 300SL continued to present challenges, especially for women with miniskirts. The bottom of the doors came only midway down the sides of the car. And with the wide sill, passengers of either sex used an entering technique that consisted of sitting on the sill and swinging their legs in and shifting to the seat in one move.

The seats now wore leather upholstery and matching fitted luggage could be ordered that could be carried in the rear.

The independent front suspension consisted of double wishbones and coil springs. It was only slightly changed from that of the 300 sedan, except that the members were drilled wherever possible for lightness. The rear axle was by swing axle and coil springs. The rear suspension was essentially unchanged from that of the sedan, except that the auxiliary torsion bars were eliminated and the shock absorbers were located behind the swing axles instead of in front.

In 1957, Mercedes-Benz introduced a Roadster version of the 300SL that was far more civilized than the coupe. The Roadster used conventional doors with a sill that was much lower and thus facilitated entry and exit. In addition, an optional hard top became available in 1958 and four-wheel disc brakes were added in 1961 as standard equipment.

Bruno Sacco says he feels that, without the hardtop, the Roadster "makes a powerful and complete impression," as opposed to the contemporary Chevrolet Corvette, which he calls "a cute vehicle with sporting appeal" that developed a design personality of its own in later years.

300SL Coupe

Wheelbase (in.)	94.5
Overall length (in.)	178.0
Overall width (in.)	70.5
Overall height (in.)	51.2
Curb weight (lb.)	2882
Engine	3.0-liter I-6
Horsepower	215 hp
Transmission	Four-speed
Top speed	159 mph

Clockwise from upper left:
The 300SL Convertible that succeeded the Gullwing Coupe exhibited the same "eyebrows" over the wheel cutouts; under the hood was a 3.0-liter inline six-cylinder engine rated at 215-hp; the Convertible used two large round dials separated by a vertical cluster housing the fuel and water temperature gauges; some people think the Convertible's styling is cleaner than the Coupe's.

Below:
With the doors closed, the 300SL Gullwing Coupe looks like a "normal" car. Only when the doors are opened is the "gullwing" feature seen.

The Roadster used heavier-gauge tubing to compensate for the absence of the coupe top. This permitted removing some of the tubes along the sides and made the use of conventional doors possible. There was a 77-pound weight penalty, however.

Under the hood, the engine received a compression ratio increase to 9.5:1, which resulted in a horsepower rating of 250.

Stirling Moss owned a production coupe. "I did a rally with it, the Tour de France," Moss remembered. "They were quite exciting cars. Not an easy car to drive, again. They were quite difficult in the wet because they didn't have the low pivot axles in the Gullwing that they did in the Roadsters. But the Gullwings were not as easy to drive as the Roadsters. The Gullwing in the wet was a very nervous, tricky car."

Incidentally, the factory never officially named the coupes "Gullwings." The name the car is known by worldwide is actually a nickname. The official name is 300SL Coupe.

In the United States, the 300SL Coupe sold originally for $6,820. The price of the Roadster at introduction was $10,970. Many people consider the Roadster to have been a superior car, even if it lacked the panache of gullwing doors. In production for seven years, the Roadster sold 1,858 units, compared with 1,400 units for the Coupe in its four-year production run.

Mercedes-Benz recognized that the 300SL was beyond the grasp of many of the people who would

Above:
Mercedes-Benz intentionally designed the economical four-cylinder 190SL to resemble the larger six-cylinder 300SL. However, the 190SL would never develop a reputation on the race track, even though many drivers competed in the car in the US.

Right:
Introduced at the New York Auto Show and urged into production by Max Hoffman, the 190SL was a "little brother" to the 300SL with more modest performance, and far more affordable.

want to buy one. In 1954, the company introduced the companion 190SL, with a 1.9-liter four-cylinder engine rated at 120 hp. The 190SL was available as a Roadster only, and had a US price of $5,020. A removable hardtop was available.

An early prototype of the 190SL debuted at the 1954 New York Auto Show, but it didn't reach production until 1955. A New York Mercedes-Benz distributor, Max Hoffman, was the angel behind the development of the car and probably sold most of the 25,881 cars that were built. Hoffman petitioned Mercedes-Benz management for a more economical sports car and promised to buy most of the production.

Like the 300SL, the 190SL was based on a production car, in this case the 180 sedan. It used the same platform, with a subframe assembly carrying the engine. It incorporated an independent front suspension and a swing-axle rear suspension, much like the 300SL.

Stylistically, the 190SL resembled the larger car, with a large oval grille dominated by the Mercedes-Benz three-pointed star. The 190SL also had "eyebrows" over the wheel arches and a "power bulge" over the inline four-cylinder engine. The sides of the 190SL were pure, though, with no engine-heat exhaust vents.

Although it never developed the competition reputation of the 300SL, the 190SL sold well, with more than 25,000 examples going to customers. Too heavy and underpowered for serious competition, it was still popular as a two-person "personal car," much in the same class as the early two-seater Ford Thunderbird and early Corvette.

The 300SLR

Mercedes-Benz returned to sports car racing in 1954 with a new car based on the 300SL. This was the 300SLR (the "R" is for racing) with a 3.0-liter straight-eight engine initially rated at 282 hp, but improved to 302 hp in 1955. While the 300SLR used the same chassis, suspension, and brakes as the 300SL, the space frame was unique.

Stirling Moss and the journalist Denis Jenkinson debuted the 300SLR at the 1955 Mille Miglia race in Italy. They won, thanks to Moss's talented driving in which he averaged almost 98 mph, aided by Jenkinson's navigation and use of a map on rollers of the entire course. Moss told the author that, although the 300SLR was powerful, it wasn't a particularly easy car to drive. "It was a great car because it was reliable and no problem from that point of view," Moss said. "But it was a large car and felt quite big. It wasn't as nimble as other cars, but it was extremely strong. It was a bit difficult in the wet."

Without Jenkinson's precise route notes, however, they could not have done as well. There were instances, Jenkinson wrote later, when Moss would crest a hill with no idea where the road went on the other side. Jenkinson would give him hand signals indicating where the road went and at what speed he could take the turn. While Moss had the 300SLR airborne a few times, they had no major problems. Moss did, however, have an accident in a road-going 300SL coupe and a training 300SLR during reconnaissance runs.

Their next time out, the 300SLRs were again victorious, with the car of Juan Manuel Fangio leading that of Moss in a 130-mile race in Sweden.

In June 1955 the 300SLRs were entered at LeMans, with three teams. Moss was leading the race with a 20-minute advantage when the 300SLR driven by Pierre Levegh ricocheted off the back of Lance Macklin's Austin-Healey and sailed into the crowd in front of the pits. The magnesium components of the Mercedes burst into flames and eventually killed 82 people, injuring more than 100.

Mercedes withdrew its team from the race early on Sunday morning as a gesture of respect for those who

had died. Moss, however, wasn't happy with the decision.

"I think it was a wrong decision, really," he said. "Obviously, the fact that we were winning affected my thoughts. But I think it was the wrong decision because it wouldn't help with the problems of the disaster that happened. I think all it really did was make a few people think that because they pulled out, maybe they had a little bit of guilt about it, which was entirely wrong. It was nothing to do with Mercedes causing the accident. They happened to be involved, but it really wasn't Mercedes' fault."

Mercedes finished the season with the 300SLRs and took the world championship. After the season ended

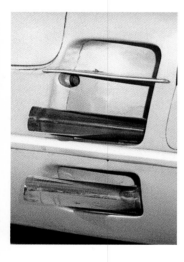

Above:
With deeper air exhausts, the 300SLR was both faster and more comfortable than the 300SL.

the company withdrew from racing until it returned in the late 1980s.

Two 300SLR coupes were built, but never competed. Known as the Uhlenhaut cars, they had longer hoods than the 300SL coupes, fared-in headlight covers, large air vents in the front fenders and huge dual exhaust pipes exiting through the air vents just in front of the passenger's door. The Mercedes-Benz historian Dennis Adler says the 300SLR coupe design "was as if the body of a 300SL coupe had been warmed and gently stretched and smoothed, with all of the hard edges blended away."

The cars were used by Uhlenhaut who, according to Moss, would arrive at races driving one of the cars.

300SLR

Wheelbase (in.)	93.3
Overall length (in.)	130.0 (est)
Overall width (in.)	66.6 (est)
Overall height (in.)	40.0 (est)
Curb weight (lb.)	2170
Engine	3.0-liter I-8
Horsepower	310 @ 7400 rpm
Transmission	Four-speed
Top speed	174 mph

Above:
Unlike the 300SL, the 300SLR was powered by an inline eight-cylinder engine. The 300SLR was the car that crashed in the 1955 Le Mans race, killing more than 80 people.

Mercedes Benz in the United States

After World War II, Mercedes-Benz cars were distributed in the United States by Max Hoffman, whose imported-car empire consisted at one time or another of Mercedes-Benz, Jaguar, BMW, Volkswagen, Porsche, Alfa Romeo, and others that have not survived to this day. Hoffman imported Mercedes cars from 1952 to 1957. His Mercedes showroom on Park Avenue in New York City was designed by Frank Lloyd Wright.

The Mercedes-Benz international export department was run by Arnold Wychodil, who believed that it was possible to improve on the small sales that Hoffman had been able to effect for the company. Carl Geise was given the assignment to expand Mercedes-Benz operations in America. He named Heinz C. Hoppe as head of the American operation. This was convenient, because Hoppe, who had first visited the United States in 1951, decided then and there that the US was where he would like to live.

Hoppe contacted Roy T. Hurley of Curtiss-Wright, which then owned Studebaker-Packard. The opportunity for increased sales was evident through Studebaker's 2,500 dealers across the country. Hoppe talked Hoffman into selling his distributorship for $2 million. The new company was to be called Curtiss-Wright and Mercedes-Benz, Inc. In September 1958, Mercedes-Benz distributorship was assumed by a new Studebaker subsidiary called Mercedes-Benz Sales Inc., located in South Bend, Indiana.

With the imminent demise of Studebaker-Packard in 1964, Mercedes-Benz bought its way out of the agreement with Curtiss-Wright, creating Mercedes-Benz of North America. Offices were originally located in Fort Lee, New Jersey, with Wychodil as titular president and Hoppe as de facto president. New headquarters were built in Montvale, New Jersey, and the headquarters relocated in 1972.

Below:
Frank Lloyd Wright designed this showroom on Park Avenue in New York City for Max Hoffman. The showroom is still in operation as one of two New York Mercedes-Benz dealerships. The spiral ramp is an excellent venue for displaying cars.

The 1960s

Mercedes 600

B y the time the 1960s had arrived, Mercedes-Benz was better able to move from producing "pedestrian" sedans alongside its marvelous sports cars and classic coupes, to returning to its roots as a producer of "grander" automobiles.

In 1938, Mercedes-Benz had introduced the seven-liter "Grosser" Mercedes 700. It was the largest car of its time and established the combined company as a builder of luxury cars on a par with Rolls-Royce.

Then came the SSK, 540K and Grand Prix-winning cars of the 1930s, followed by the devastation of World War II. After the 300SL returned Mercedes-Benz to the pinnacle of sports car racing, and Juan Manuel Fangio and Stirling Moss brought Grand Prix glory back with the Silver Arrows, it was time for a new "Grosser."

600 Pullman	
Wheelbase (in.)	153.5
Overall length (in.)	245.7
Overall width (in.)	76.8
Overall height (in.)	63.0
Curb weight (lb.)	5830
Engine	6.3-liter V-8
Horsepower	250 @ 4000 rpm
Transmission	Four-speed automatic
Top speed	125 mph

So Mercedes-Benz came out with the Pullman. Introduced at Frankfurt in 1963, the 600 was powered by a 300 (SAE) hp 6.3-liter V8 with fuel injection and

Clockwise from upper left:
The 600 Pullman interior offered full leather upholstery; rear legroom was exceptional, and the car offered jump seats for extra passengers; access to both front and rear seats was excellent; the driving compartment was "standard" Mercedes-Benz; the rear seats reclined for added comfort.

an overhead camshaft for each bank of cylinders. The 600 could accelerate from 0-62 mph in 10 seconds and hit a top speed of 127 mph despite its size.

The 600 was available in two body styles, a six-passenger "limousine" sedan on a 126-inch wheelbase or an eight-passenger Pullman limousine on a 153.5-inch wheelbase. The Pullman was 246 inches long overall, more than 20 feet, in an era when the largest Cadillac was "only" 220 inches long.

Size wasn't the only determinant in establishing the reputation of this newest "Grosser." The 600 was also equipped with an air suspension and automatic adjustable shock absorbers, four-wheel disc brakes, a four-speed automatic transmission, power steering, dual zone heating and air conditioning, adjustable steering wheel and central locking for the doors and trunk lid.

When the 600 reached the US in May 1964, the sedan sold for $19,500 and the Pullman for $24,000. These prices rose to $23,580 and $26,953, respectively, by October 1969. The 600 remained on the market until 1981, with a total of 2,190 sedans and 487 Pullmans built.

So which was best? Mercedes built a car that was bigger than a Cadillac and more opulent than a Rolls-Royce. How did it stack up against the competition?

Popular Science did a comparison test in its February 1967 issue. While not a direct head-to-head comparison, the magazine asked three of its reporters an intriguing question: "If you had $1,000,000 which car would you buy? A Caddy? Rolls? Mercedes? Obviously, Devon Francis, *PS* European Editor David Scott and *PS* Automotive Editor Jan Norbye had differing opinions.

Francis chose the front-wheel drive 1967 Cadillac Eldorado. As the world's only car (at that time) "with a combination of front-wheel drive, variable ratio power steering and automatic leveling as standard, it had a wheelbase of 120 inches and overall length of 221 inches." It weighed 4,647 pounds and was powered by a 429 cubic inch (7.0 liters) V8 developing 340 hp. Francis was able to "squeal rubber on takeoff," but the automatic leveling kept the lights on the road regardless of the load being carried.

"Practically everything ... is automatic," Francis wrote. "If I had any bleats on this job, it was only on the sparse headroom; inside, finger-catching door releases."

Scott chose a Rolls-Royce Silver Shadow with a 380.5 cubic inch (6.2 liters) V8 rated at approximately 285 hp. "You, too," he wrote, "would like the electric control of the automatic transmission. There are no linkage complications, and you get immediate shifts. You don't look under the hood for oil and water levels. There are warning lights for that. There's also a light that goes on when you're down to three gallons of fuel and a hand-brake light that goes on in case of burned-out stoplights."

Norbye's choice was the Mercedes 600. "This car was designed to be the finest automobile ever built in regular production, regardless of cost. You can tell it's something special before you even get inside. An effortless touch of the handle opens the door. And the door helps shut itself – quietly, with hydraulic power."

Norbye lauded the fit and finish of the 600. "Nothing is loose. You don't even see mismatched joints in rubber moldings. Nothing looks added on; all accessories are built in. The finish is superb, there's no end to its refinements."

As in all such tests, there was no conclusive decision. At $21,000, the Mercedes was $1,300 more expensive than the Rolls and more than twice the price of the Caddy. It deserved to win.

The early SLs

The 190SL achieved greater commercial success than the 300SL before it, with 25,881 cars built before production ended in February 1963. The four-cylinder Roadster never received the same critical acclaim as its bigger brother, however it did offer Mercedes-Benz sportiness in an economical package that was within the financial reach (and driving ability) of far more people.

190SL

Wheelbase (in.)	94.5
Overall length (in.)	166.1
Overall width (in.)	68.5
Overall height (in.)	52.0
Curb weight (lb.)	2376
Engine	1.9-liter I-4
Horsepower	105 hp @ 5700 rpm/
Transmission	Four-speed
Top speed	107 mph

Above:
The 190SL shared many of the design cues of the 300SL; simple grille dominated by a three-pointed star, "eyebrows" over the wheel arches, a "power bulge" in the hood, and sleek, aerodynamic styling.

230 SL	
Wheelbase (in.)	94.5
Overall length (in.)	168.7
Overall width (in.)	69.3
Overall height (in.)	51.2
Curb weight (lb.)	2849
Engine	2.3-liter I-6
Horsepower	150 @ 5500 rpm
Transmission	Four-speed manual/ three-speed automatic
Top speed	122 mph

The successor to the 190SL was the 230SL, introduced in March 1963 at Geneva. Here was a car with a six-cylinder engine like the 300SL, but with the manners and handling of the 190SL. It was a compromise, but indicated the direction Mercedes-Benz sports cars would go in the future.

The 230SL used the underpinnings of the 220 sedan, with a shortened floor pan and slightly larger engine. The wheelbase was 94.5 inches and the overall length was 169.6 inches. The 2.2-liter engine of the 220 sedan received a 2-mm larger bore, increasing capacity to 2,306 cc. It produced 150 net horsepower using intermittent fuel injection, in which injection takes place in the intake duct of the cylinder head, preheated by radiator coolant.

Underneath, the 230SL used an independent front suspension and a 3.75:1 rear swing axle using a single joint with a low pivot point and a compensating coil spring. At the front were double wishbones and coil springs. Mechanically, the 230SL was the work of Josef Muller, who became chief passenger car engineer in 1956, replacing Hans Scherenberg, who had succeeded Fritz Nallinger.

The most interesting feature of the 230SL was its tall windows and "pagoda" hardtop roof. Paul Bracq is credited with the unique design. The tall windows created a larger door opening, which made entering and exiting the 230SL much easier than in the 190SL.

Far left:
The second-generation SL series was initiated by the 230SL, with a 2.3-liter six-cylinder engine. Front styling was highlighted by vertical headlights, while the side windows were large, resulting in easier access.

Above:
Drivers and passengers had this view of the 230SL dash. Note the padded steering wheel and padded dash for safety. Instruments included a large tachometer and speedometer. The four-speed transmission had a long shift lever.

Obviously, visibility was also improved. To keep the overall height of the car as low as possible with either the soft or hard top installed, however, a central depression was created that lowered the roof by an inch or so. This gave it the classic concave, or "pagoda" shape.

"It is very difficult to classify our 230SL Roadster of 1963," Bruno Sacco wrote in *Mercedes-Benz Design*. "It is an attempt to replace the legendary SL Roadster and the weakly styled 190SL with a single successor – a successor with dubious styling yet remarkable success. The pagoda roof is the outstanding styling element, which, unusual though it is, was based on a functional consideration, namely to provide more headroom for passengers when getting in and out. The pagoda roof was not adopted by any other manufacturer. The somewhat coquettish appearance of this car, which was

especially appealing to women, caused a shift away from the image of our sports car – far away from the 300SL."

Many complained about the 230SL's lack of "sportiness." However, *Autocar*'s 1964 road test concluded, "With an extra inch beyond the 190SL, the wide track helps toward neutral balance and superb adhesion which are the car's outstanding qualities. Corners can be taken at almost prodigious speeds with extraordinary stability, ease of mind and control, and there is almost no apparent body sway to emphasize how hard the car is being cornered."

Still, there were naysayers. After all, this wasn't another 300SL. Mercedes-Benz responded by entering a 230SL in the 1963 Spa–Sofia–Liége Rally, the prodigious Marathon de la Route. Driven by Eugen Bôhringer, the car won, establishing its credentials. It may have been the first time a car with an automatic transmission and power steering had been so successful in motor-sport competition, even if it wasn't a pure race.

In 1967, Mercedes-Benz introduced a larger-engined version of the 230SL, the 250SL, with a 2,496-cc version of the six-cylinder engine. Only 5,196 copies of this car were built before Mercedes again increased

engine capacity, creating the 280SL in January 1968. This car was the most successful of the three in the series, with 23,885 examples built.

The 280SL's 2,778-cc engine produced 170 net horsepower. The US version delivered 180 SAE horsepower and could move the 280SL from 0–60 mph in 10 seconds. The transmission was a four-speed

Below:
With a slightly larger engine, the 250SL replaced the 230SL in the second-generation SL lineup. Both cars exhibited large side windows that were necessary for easier access to the car.

Above:
The tall windows of the 250SL, combined with a lower center-section of the optional hardtop (and convertible top), gave the second-series SLs their identifying "Pagoda" roof.

Right:
While most sports cars of the era were leaning toward high-maintenance wire wheels, the 250SL instead used simple disc wheel design.

automatic, but a five-speed ZF manual was optionally available, if rarely fitted.

Ian Fraser, writing in the Mercedes-Benz Club of America's publication, *The Star*, wrote, "Somewhere along the way, Mercedes lost their way in the gear-change department. I was shocked to find that the [230SL's] lever was the antithesis of the 300SL's: imprecise, wobbly, vague. In fact, after the 300SL, Mercedes never again made a car with a good manual gear-change; that's why the automatics are so popular."

These cars were not 300SL sports cars, despite Bôhringer's success in the Marathon. They were luxury grand tourers, with air conditioning, automatic transmissions, leather seats, and real-glass windows.

Pininfarina executed a one-off fixed coupe variation of the 280SL in 1965. The car has classic Pininfarina styling and resembles Ferrari coupes of the same era.

250SL

Wheelbase (in.)	94.5
Overall length (in.)	168.7
Overall width (in.)	69.3
Overall height (in.)	51.2
Curb weight (lb.)	2992
Engine	2.5-liter I-6
Horsepower	150 @ 5500 rpm
Transmission	Four-speed automatic
Top speed	122 mph

While the dash remained the same, Pininfarina redid the interior as well as the exterior, creating an unusual variation of an already excellent car.

Mercedes replaced the 280SL in April 1971 with the 350SL, an all-new car with a 3.5-liter V8 engine. This car looked bold and bulky, too bulky for some, with a definite wedge profile. The wheelbase was 96.7 inches, just slightly longer than the preceding series. Suspension geometry had changed, though, with parallel wishbones in front and trailing arms in the rear.

A few months later, Mercedes-Benz came out with the 350SLC coupe, a fixed-hardtop version of the SL on a 110.8-inch wheelbase. The longer wheelbase softened the stubbiness of the Roadster and gave it smoother lines.

Above:
Second series SLs were available with six-cylinder engines as large as 2.8 liters, as in this 280SL. The cars are noted not only for the "Pagoda" roof but for their rectangular lines and simplicity of design.

Left:
Sports cars, even Mercedes-Benz sports cars, are meant to be seen with their tops down. The 280SL presents a particularly clean package with no bulge above the body line where the top recessed.

280SL

Wheelbase (in.)	94.5
Overall length (in.)	168.7
Overall width (in.)	69.3
Overall height (in.)	51.2
Curb weight (lb.)	3113
Engine	2.8-liter I-6
Horsepower	170 @ 5750 rpm
Transmission	Four-speed automatic
Top speed	122 mph

Far right:
Inside, the 280SL dash retained some of the styling cues of the 300SL convertible; a large speedometer and tachometer flanking a vertical array of accessory instruments. Note the padded steering wheel hub.

Below:
The 280SL represented the last of Mercedes-Benz sports cars that were "Sport" and "Light." Later, SLs would be bulker and heavier.

This "third series" of SL cars was the most popular and had the most engine options. After the original 350SL and SLC came the 450SL and SLC, although US versions of the car had the 4.5-liter V8 under 350SL nomenclature. After the 450 came the reincarnation of the 280SL and SLC with a double-overhead-cam version of the 2,746-cc six. In 1981, Americans received the 380SL with a 3.8-liter, 155-hp V8. The United States was in the midst of reaction to two fuel crises and renewed attention to exhaust pollution. All cars had emasculated power figures.

In Europe, Mercedes introduced in 1978 the 450SLC 5.0, with a 5.0-liter V8 engine developing 240 hp. These cars were the factory rally cars and delivered several international successes to Mercedes-Benz in the late 1970s and 1980s. While they were not officially imported to the US, "gray market" versions of the cars did enter the company through Canadian outlets. The last of the series to be officially imported to the United States was the 560SL, with a 5.6-liter V8 engine. With fuel injection, this engine delivered 227 horsepower and 279 foot-pounds of torque. Top speed was 130 mph and it would accelerate from 0–60 mph in 7.5 seconds.

The last of the R107 series of cars was built on August 4, 1989, in Bremen and was delivered to the Mercedes-Benz Museum in Stuttgart. It was a 560SL.

Writing in *Car Collector* in 1978, Karl Ludvigsen says,

> Even without the added half liter, even with the emissions hardware that throttles modern engines, the 450SL is a car with immensely satisfying performance. Pressure on the right-hand pedal moves it ahead with a muffled roar of authority. Its controls respond with delicacy and precision. It is satisfying in other ways. It upholds the Sindlefingen traditions with the look and feel of coach-built craftsmanship. [It leaves] the impression of purposeful care in construction that evokes memories of the 300SL, the 500K and the SSK. [It reminds] us of the heritage of magnificent grand touring cars that remains vitally alive at Daimler-Benz.

Left and below:
Third-generation SLs entered the world with a 4.5-liter V-8 engine in the 450SL. The 450SL was also available as a fixed-roof coupe, but as with its predecessors, it is best known as a roadster or convertible.

450SL

Wheelbase (in.)	96.7
Overall length (in.)	187.0
Overall width (in.)	70.5
Overall height (in.)	52.4
Curb weight (lb.)	3487
Engine	4.5-liter V-8
Horsepower	226 @ 5000 rpm
Transmission	Three-speed automatic
Top speed	119 mph

The C111

One of the most exciting Mercedes-Benz models of all time was never a production model, although if the company had chosen to build it in series it could have sold several hundred at enormous profit. The car is the C111, and was used primarily by Mercedes as a test bed for engine development and record-setting.

The first of five C111 cars was completed on April 1, 1969. It was blessed with wedge-shaped styling and a huge rectangular grille with an enormous three-pointed star in the center, leaving no doubt as to what kind of car it was. Interestingly, this grille served as an air outlet rather than an air inlet.

Like the 300SL before it, the C111 was equipped with gullwing doors that hinged in the center of the roof. Originally, the car was called C101, but when it came close to production it was realized that Peugeot had a license on all cars' model names with a zero as the middle digit. So the C101 became the C111.

C111-I

Wheelbase (in.)	103.1
Overall length (in.)	165.4
Overall width (in.)	70.9
Overall height (in.)	44.3
Curb weight (lb.)	2530
Engine	1.8-liter three-rotor Wankel
Horsepower	300 @ 7000 rpm
Transmission	Five-speed manual
Top speed	165 mph

Left:
With dramatic wedge styling that was the modern equivalent of the 300SL Gullwing Coupe, the C111 project car also used gullwing doors on a clean aerodynamic body.

Mercedes-Benz always considered the C111 as a traveling laboratory. Its first engine was a three-rotor Wankel rotary engine that was rated at 300 hp. It had a top speed of 167 mph. The Wankel engine was originally planned for the 350SLC coupe, but it never made it into production because the Wankel rotary never achieved the fuel economy figures that were expected of it.

Rudolf Uhlenhaut was the development manager for the car and it was he who took it on its first test drive on the highway. After the first car was built, five additional examples were built. One of these was shown at the 1969 Frankfurt Auto Show and became the hit of the show. Several people sent blank checks to Stuttgart in the hope of buying one of these cars, and at least one American racer is known to have been willing to "sell my soul" if he could own one. But the cars never went on sale. Even Felix Wankel, the designer of the engine, was unable to convince Daimler-Benz that he deserved one of the cars.

The three-rotor Wankel engine was located just ahead of the rear wheels and drove the wheels through a five-speed transmission. When Mercedes decided the three-rotor engine wouldn't do the job intended for it, a four-rotor engine was developed. This engine developed 350 hp and was shoehorned into prototype five, earning the designation C111-II. Already blessed with an outstanding coefficient of drag (Cd), the new car was changed slightly to improve this figure to 0.325. C111-II weighed 2,728 pounds and could reach 62 mph in 4.8 seconds. Top speed was 186 mph. This car was shown at the 1970 Geneva Motor Show and was the first of eight C111-IIs built.

C111-II was a car that was as close to a production car that Mercedes-Benz could have developed. The interior was well finished with a full complement of instruments and upholstery on the seats. Even the steering wheel was a production item. To show that the ventilation around the engine was good and that the insulation between it and the luggage tray worked, Mercedes engineers placed two suitcases in the luggage compartments during some of the testing.

In 1970, Mercedes-Benz's public-affairs director, Heinz Schmidt, offered four possible scenarios for the future of the C111.

1. It could be built in limited quantities of 100 to 500 units a year.
2. It could be officially withdrawn by the end of 1971.
3. It could be further developed as an experimental vehicle.
4. A small series of 30 to 50 could be built and loaned to drivers for test purposes, much in the same way Chrysler loaned turbine cars to test-drivers during the 1960s.

Further development of the C111 was eventually limited by the first Arab oil crisis, which focused the company's attention on an engine that did deliver the kind of economy that was needed in those times. This was the diesel engine.

Mercedes-Benz thus put a 190-hp, five-cylinder, diesel engine with a Garrett turbocharger into one of the C111-II models and took it to the Nardo racing circuit in southern Italy. With this engine the C111-II broke 16 diesel records including three new world records. Acceleration was also excellent, with 100 km (62 mph) being reached in 6.8 seconds.

Early in 1977, C111-III began taking shape in the styling department at Sindlefingen. This car achieved a new Cd of 0.183 and had fared-in wheels, a longer, lower body, and a single vertical air foil at the rear.

Once again the car was taken to the 7.8-mile Nardo circuit. Top speeds for the C111-III were more than 205 mph. In 12 hours, nine new world records were broken. The drivers were Guido Moch, Paul Frère, Dr Hans Liebold, and Rico Steinemann.

Buoyed by the success of this car, Mercedes-Benz brought the original C111 back and renamed it C111-IV. The goal was to break the closed-circuit record set by Mark Donohue at Talladega in a Porsche 917/30. Donohue's record was 220.6 mph.

For an engine, Mercedes installed a 5.0-liter V8 and attached two KKK turbochargers, giving 500 horsepower at 6,200 rpm. Spoilers on the car were designed asymmetrically, since the cars always run in a circle at Nardo. The Cd was lowered slightly to 0.182. Nine world records were set in May 1979, including the desired one, a new closed-circuit record of 250.918 mph. Hans Liebold was the driver. The Mercedes-Benz record is even more impressive when you realize that the engine developed 500 hp to Donohue's 1,000 hp. In fairness, though, Donohue's car was a Can Am car while the Mercedes-Benz was purpose-built to set speed records.

Competition

When Mercedes-Benz withdrew from racing at the close of the 1955 season, one of the great names in competition was no longer active. However, with Karl Kling and his successor Baron von Korff working as manager of the motorsports operation, Mercedes-Benz did not withdraw completely from motorsports. The new venue was international rallying, and as long as production-based cars were the vehicles to be used in competition, Mercedes-Benz was willing to be at the starting line.

Mercedes-Benz had competed in rallies during the 1950s, in particular the Monte Carlo and Liège–Rome–Liège. As Karl Ludvigsen wrote in *Quicksilver Century,*

"They were finishers rather than winners."

In 1960, however, that would change. Kling entered a team of 220SE sedans in the Monte Carlo Rally that year. The three Mercedes-Benz team cars took the top three positions, led by Walter Schock and Rolf Moll. Eugen Bôhringer and Herman Socher finished second and Rolant Ott and Eberhard Mahle third. Schock and Moll also won the Acropolis Rally and earned enough points to take the European Rally Championship.

In 1961, the company entered four 220SE sedans in the Argentine Gran Premio Standard, a 2,756-mile production-car race from Buenos Aires to Chile and back. Schock won, followed by Hans Hermann.

Below:
In recent years, the "factory" racing effort has been undertaken by the AMG company. This car is a C-Class sedan prepared by AMG to run in the German Touring Car Championships.

Ewy Rosqvist and Ursula Wirth won the Gran Premio in 1962, and Bôhringer won it in 1963 and 1964 in a 300SE sedan. Bôhringer tried circuit racing in 1964, winning his class in the 300SE at Brands Hatch in England. He retired in 1965.

But before he retired, Bôhringer won the 1963 Liège–Sofia–Liège rally in a 230SL, repeating his win of 1962 in a 220SE. Bôhringer also won the European Rally championship in 1962.

During the 1970s, Mercedes-Benz prepared coupe versions of its SL sports cars for rally competition and had success worldwide.

Mercedes-Benz's enviable rally record came to an end in 1991. At a victory celebration following the finish of the Ivory Coast Rally, the company announced that it was ceasing participation in rallies for the foreseeable future. The reason given was that the company's resources would be better focused on complying with the sharp acceleration in legislative and environmental demands being placed on the automobile.

Its research head, Werner Breitschwerdt, also admitted that the company's then current line of cars was ill-suited to European rallies. Daimler-Benz would like to have developed a special car for rallying, as Peugeot, among others, was doing, but the development capacity for the effort was simply not there.

In 1961, Mercedes introduced the 220SE, with the S denoting "Super" and the E "Einspritzung," or fuel injected. The 220SE eschewed the finned rear fenders of the 220, introduced in 1959. Mercedes-Benz had had its fling with styling trends and would now return to the conservative styling (for a while) that had served it so well in the past and would continue to serve it well in the future. As the historian W. Robert Nitske noted in *Mercedes-Benz: Production Models Book 1946–1995*, "The body styles of the convertible and coupe were more modern – the rear fins were eliminated and the edge slightly rounded – and the cars were much more luxuriously equipped. Real leather upholstery was standard and a four-speed automatic transmission with floor-mounted shift lever, as well as a tachometer, were standard equipment of these truly elegant automobiles."

With a 2.2-liter, fuel-injected, six-cylinder engine developing 134 SAE horsepower, the 220SE could reach a top speed of 107 mph.

The 220SE begat the 300SE of 1961, with a 3.0-liter overhead camshaft six, rated at 185 horsepower. Top speed had improved to 124 mph. An air suspension system and four-wheel disc brakes were standard on the 300SE. A year after the introduction of the *finned* sedan came a non-finned coupe and convertible. A year after that, in March 1963, a long-wheelbase model was added. Where the original 300SE rode on a 108.3-inch wheelbase, the "long" had a 112.2-inch wheelbase.

In 1965, as the first SEs were coming to the end of their production runs, Mercedes-Benz brought out the 250SE, which was a fuel-injected version of the 250S introduced at Frankfurt in 1965. Tail fins were gone for good and the cars had a lower waistline and larger window area than the previous 220 series cars. The roof was also flatter, although not concave like the SL sports coupes. In the suspension area, the 250SE had a reinforced rear axle with a hydropneumatic compensating spring.

Big brother to the 250SE was the 300SE. But the 300SE itself had a bigger brother, the 300SEL, with the L denoting "long" for its wheelbase, which was 100 millimeters or 3.9 inches longer. The SEL used the air suspension system that was shared by the coupe and convertible models of the 300SE. The 3.0-liter six was rated at 195 SAE horsepower, which, with the proper rear axle ratio, could move the 300SE to 124 mph.

In the United States, Mercedes-Benz introduced the 300SEL 6.3 at Laguna Seca in California. Rudolf Uhlenhaut was at the introduction and pointed out that the car had better road-holding ability, braking potential, suspension stability, and maneuverability than any comparable automobile in the world. Under the hood was a 6.3-liter overhead camshaft V8 that developed 300 SAE horsepower. This engine was originally designed to propel the 600 Pullman. Putting it in the smaller 300SEL body was akin to stuffing a 427 Ford engine in a Pinto. Top speed was 137 mph. It

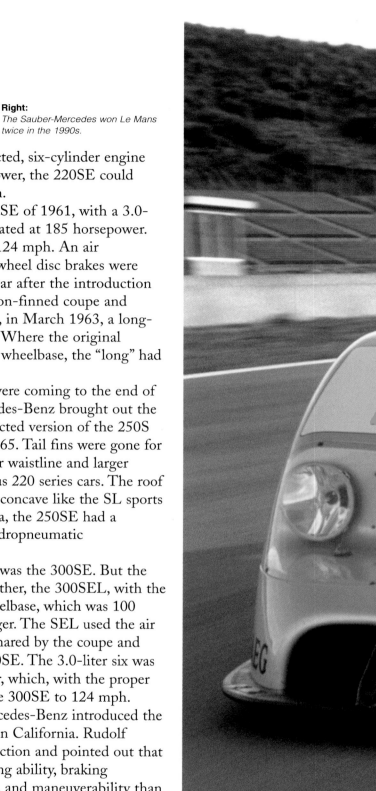

Right:
The Sauber-Mercedes won Le Mans twice in the 1990s.

could accelerate from 0–60 mph in 6.5 seconds. Here was a mighty automobile.

Car and Driver called the 300SEL 6.3 "the most stimulating, desirable 4-door sedan to appear since the Model J Duesenberg." *Road & Track* called it "The greatest sedan in the world."

The 300SEL 6.3 weighed more than 3,800 pounds and came fully equipped with a four-speed automatic transmission, air conditioning, air suspension system, power brakes, power steering, walnut trim, and crushed-velour upholstery.

The standard 300SEL carried the 3.0-liter overhead camshaft six, which was rated at 180 hp. It had a short production life, heightened by the fact that the 6.3 outsold it in 1969.

Supplanting the 300SEL was the 300SEL 3.5 with a 3.5-liter V8 developing 230 SAE horsepower. With the new M116 engine, it sold 1,039 units in the United States of the 9,483 total sales.

The Mercedes-Benz nomenclature was obviously undergoing great stress, with engine sizes changing (seemingly) constantly. There was the 300SEL 6.3, the 300SEL 3.5, the "normal" 300SEL, a 280SEL 4.5 with the 4.5-liter V8, and a 300SEL 4.5 with the same engine. The differences between the 280SEL 4.5 and the 300SEL 4.5 were relatively minor. The 280SEL was 10 mm (less than half an inch) wider and the 300SEL was 250 pounds heavier. The 300SEL was more luxurious, making it, as one writer said, "the very best of the top line."

Below:
The most recent Mercedes-Benz prototype sports car racer is the CLK-GTR, with a 6.0-liter V-12 engine and front-end styling that would surface on the later production E-Class

The 1970s and 1980s

Previous page:
The 500SE represented Mercedes-Benz's largest true production car through the 1970s and 1980s. With a 5.0-liter V-8 engine, it would evolve into the modern S-Class.

Right:
With the SL sports cars came fixed-roof coupes that were less sporting but offered luxury and comfort along with two-seater sportiness.

Below:
For years, the best-selling Mercedes-Benz has been the C-Class. The 220 is the ancestor of the modern C.

Mercedes-Benz, like most European manufacturers, was not a slave to the calendar when it introduced new-model automobiles. In the United States, the annual new-model change was a ritual, and the first day the new models would be exhibited at dealerships was an exciting one. Windows would be covered with brown paper and no one would be permitted to get even a glance at the new models until the magic day arrived. When the big day came, the paper was ceremoniously torn off the windows and people could see what the designers at Ford, or Chevrolet, or Cadillac, or Chrysler had wrought.

European manufacturers, on the other hand, tended to introduce new models when it was time to introduce a new model. It might be in April or August, rather than the traditional September or October favored by their American cousins.

This is all well and good for manufacturers and car buyers. Car historians, on the other hand, like to place the objects of their study in time capsules. Ten-year capsules are the neatest, representing the decades of a company's life. Mercedes-Benz simply would not cooperate. We will see with the next group of cars, whose introduction and production lasted over the period of approximately 15 years.

The G-Wagen

In 1973, a completely new vehicle joined the Mercedes-Benz lineup. It was the Gelandewagen, or G-Wagen, a four-wheel-drive off-road vehicle that was a sport utility vehicle before the sport utility craze. Originally developed for military use, the G-Wagen was later "civilized" for non-military use. It found a home in such diverse environments as country club parking lots as well as in off-road environments.

As Michael Lamm wrote in *M-Class*, "Originally designed for military use, the G-Wagen is a wonder car for anyone with off-road aspirations because of its numerous desirable traits. Like being able to shift between high and low gear ranges in the transfer case while moving, or electronically locking the center, rear and, finally, the front differential for the ultimate in traction. And because even an off-road Mercedes-Benz is still part of the family, the interior is beautifully finished with the options of polished wood trim and leather upholstery."

But, as Lamm continued, the fall of the Berlin Wall and the easing of East-West tensions reduced the demand for military vehicles. The G-Wagen's development was shifted to the passenger car division. Studies were begun to determine its usefulness in the early 1990s, headed by a young engineer, Andreas Renschler. But that story is best left to the section on the M-Class.

The G-Wagen was first offered with a choice of a 2.4-liter diesel engine or 2.8- or 2.3-liter gasoline engine. Later, a 3.0-liter diesel engine was offered as was a higher-performance 2.3-liter gasoline engine. The most powerful of these was the fuel-injected 280GE, with 156 horsepower. The injected 230GE of 1982 was second in power with 125 hp, far ahead of the traditionally modest diesel-engined vehicles.

Gelandewagens were built in collaboration with the Austrian Puch-Werken. Mercedes-Benz didn't go overboard in the styling of these utility vehicles. They are a cross between a Land Rover and Jeep Grand Cherokee, with slab sides and a decidedly vertical

appearance. It wasn't until the AAV show vehicle that Mercedes-Benz let its designers loose on designing a sport utility vehicle.

Still, the G-Wagens were comfortable on road and practical off-road. The dash was plain and functional, with a center console housing the sound and HVAC controls and an instrument pod in front of the driver with speedometer, tachometer, accessory gauges and a readout telling the driver which drive mode is in use.

Between the seats, the center console housed a four-speed manual gearbox, auxiliary transmission for the transfer case and limited slip differential controls. Seats were functionally cloth-covered in a pattern that would remind one of the original 300SL Gullwing, but leather was an option.

The box-section chassis was offered in two wheelbases, 94.5 and 112.2 inches, with overall lengths a mere 155.3 and 173.0 inches, respectively. Tires were 205/16 radials. While the G-Wagen served its purpose well, and some are still in use on US ranches, it was superseded by the M-Series in 1996.

Above:
Conceived and designed as a military vehicle, the Gelandewagen, or G-Wagen, had full off-road capability but no panache. Its successor, the M-Class, has panache.

Birth of the C-Class

While Mercedes-Benz has earned a well-deserved reputation for creating automotive masterpieces, it is in its regular production cars where the company has shone through the decades. In the late 1990s, the C-Class cars have been the force that has propelled Mercedes-Benz into profitability and high-volume production. These vehicles show their heritage in the W123 chassis cars that were first introduced in 1976.

Known at the time as the Type 200, for its 2.0-liter four-cylinder engine, the W123 platform cars had a myriad of identifications. Among the models built on the platform were the original 1976 200; the 1980 200 with a slightly larger, more powerful engine; the 1976 230; the 1980 230E with fuel injection and more power; the 1976 six-cylinder 250; the 1976 280E with a 177-hp 2.8-liter DOHC six-cylinder engine; the diesel-engined 1976 200D, 220D, 240D, and 300D. Also built on this platform were the station wagons – 200T, 230T, 230TE, 250T, 280TE, 240TD, 300TD. A coupe version of the sedan body yielded the 230C, 230CE, 280C, 280CE, and 300CD. That's twenty-two models built off the same platform. No wonder Daimler-Benz

was attracted by Chrysler in 1997, since Chrysler got so much mileage out of its K Car platform.

These cars proved to be Daimler-Benz's most popular cars ever, with total sales in excess of 2.2 million vehicles. The reasons for the success are simple; build a good chassis, clothe it with a conservative, timeless body, and keep changing the engines as technology advances.

Interiors of the W123 models were conservative as well. Cloth upholstery was standard, but leather facing could be ordered. Legroom was adequate front and rear, enough so that the car formed the basis for German taxicab fleets.

After a run of more than ten years, the W124 cars were replaced by the W201 cars, also known as the 190 series because of the engine size of the most economical model. Again, conservative styling was a keynote of these models.

The 190 in its most basic form was powered by a 1.9-liter four-cylinder engine rated at 90 hp. Fuel injection raised the power to 122 hp in Europe and 115 hp in the United States.

The 190E was also available with an engine that had been tuned by Cosworth Engineering to deliver 185 horsepower. With a deep front spoiler, a small rear spoiler on the trunk lid, and special tires, the 190E, 2.3-16 had a top speed of more than 130 mph. The speedometer's top reading was 260kph and the 190E, 2.3-16 was only available with a five-speed manual gearbox. The car was a preview of AMG-tuned cars that Mercedes-Benz would sell in the 1990s.

Other versions of the 201 were the diesel-engined 190D and 190D2.5 (a 2.5-liter five-cylinder version).

A new base class Mercedes appeared in 1985, the W124 200, with a 2.0-liter 104-hp four-cylinder engine. Again, it was conservatively styled, but in breaking new ground and showing an evolution from previous Mercedes-Benz models, it proved to be a car that would, like the W123 models, sell in the millions.

Slightly larger than the base 200 was the 230E, with a fuel-injected 2.3-liter four rated at 136 hp. The 260E offered 170 hp and the 300E 190. These two cars were sold in the United States as the 300E2.6 and 300E24, respectively.

They would eventually evolve into the C-Class vehicles in the mid 1990s, when Mercedes-Benz chose to rename their vehicles.

Mercedes-Benz didn't abandon its luxury car roots, however. In 1985, at the Frankfurt Auto Show, MB introduced the 260SE, on the W196 platform. This was

Above:
The largest engine available in a C-Class was the 3.0-liter turbocharged five-cylinder diesel of the 300TD.

the first "S-Class" sedan, a larger, more luxurious version of the base sedan, with outstanding front and rear legroom and amenities that could please anyone. While not in the same class as the 600, the S-Class was and continues to be the ultimate in Mercedes-Benz sedans.

As is the pattern with Mercedes-Benz, the S-Class was available with a variety of different engines. The 260SE was powered by a 2.6-liter six; the 300SE and SEL (long wheelbase version) used a 180-hp 3.0-liter six; the 420 SE and SEL were powered by a 4.2-liter V8 that put out 218 hp; and the 500SE and SEL's 5.0-liter V8 was capable of 245 hp. The ultimate "first edition" S-Class was the 560SEL with a 300 hp V8. It was only available in the long-wheelbase version.

Station Wagons

At the 1977 Frankfurt Auto Show, Mercedes-Benz introduced the T series of cars, T meaning "Touristik and Transport," or station wagon. Long before minivans and sport utilities, station wagons were the cars for practical families. They offered more cargo capacity than a standard sedan, while still offering the handling of a sedan and much of the performance.

The first of these models was the 240TD, with a 2.4-liter four-cylinder diesel engine rated at 72 hp. Mercedes would show two diesel-engined models and three gasoline-engined models at Frankfurt.

These were the first wagons for Mercedes-Benz, although custom body manufacturers had built wagons and "shooting brakes" on Mercedes chassis over the years. Based on the W123 sedan line, the wagons shared many components with these cars.

The 300TD had the same engine as the 300D, which had been introduced a year earlier. This was a five-cylinder diesel and was the first five-cylinder engine in modern production. Produced for five years, the 300D was the most popular diesel-engined car in the United States. In 1982 it was replaced by a

turbo diesel model. Output for the normally aspirated engine was 77 SAE hp originally. The turbo reached 120 hp.

Mercedes went to great lengths at the introduction of the five-cylinder to show that the harmonics of a five-cylinder were only slightly inferior to those of the six-cylinder, which was the ideal configuration. Why did Mercedes go to five instead of six cylinders, then? It was a matter of economics and weight. The 240D four-cylinder diesel was slightly underpowered, especially in the United States, which was Mercedes' largest market. Adding two cylinders would have made the engine too heavy and would have required more substantial changes to the suspension to handle the extra weight. Adding one cylinder, though, would increase power by 25 percent with only a minimal increase in engine weight.

The station wagon had the same interior as in the sedan version. A manually operated sunroof was available. In the back, the rear gate opened up like a hatch. The storage area was 48 inches long by 58 inches wide. The length could be extended to 70 inches, giving a cargo volume of 45.9 cubic feet with the rear seat folded. Removing the rear seat extended the load carrying length to almost 80 inches. The passenger seat could also be removed to carry extra-long objects. An automatic self-leveling device was included on the rear suspension.

T-series vehicles were additionally available with gasoline engines, including the 2.3-liter four, a fuel-injected 2.3-liter four with 27 more DIN horsepower, a 2.5-liter six, and a 2.8-liter fuel-injected six, offering 185 DIN hp.

Transmissions in the wagons were a four-speed manual gearbox as standard, with the option of a four-speed automatic also available.

Above:
Mercedes-Benz has continued to build station wagons along with its sedans, coupes and sports cars. This 300TE wagon is powered by a 3.0-liter inline six-cylinder engine.

The Fourth Generation SL

Work began on a new generation of SL two-seaters in 1982. The goal was to restore style and elegance to the SL range on the one hand and to simplify what had become a confusing array of models on the other.

Bruno Sacco led the design team working on the new cars, which would be designated R129. The design team's charter was to create a design that would be equally attractive with the top up or down. The engineering department at Mercedes-Benz had created a mechanical soft top that could be raised or lowered in a matter of seconds simply by pushing a button on the console between the seats.

The top proved to be a particular challenge. A final design was approved only after 34 different designs were considered. The result was an aerodynamic and watertight convertible that looked good when it rained and whose top would retract into a compartment behind the passenger compartment.

With an emphasis on safety, the top also had to make provision for the rollover bar that would activate if sensors determined a possible rollover situation. The bar would activate if the top was raised or lowered.

Three different design philosophies were considered: a continuation of the present cars; a more futuristic design but still with classic SL design elements; and a development of the SL theme in a more homogeneous design. The third approach is the one that was followed.

As with many Mercedes-Benz designs, the final one chosen for the SL was conservative, not radical; evolutionary, not revolutionary. With only four different designs in the 35 years from the first 300SL to the newest, a radical change would not hold up well in the marketplace. Bruno Alfieri, who wrote a book on the

Below:
With its 6.0-liter V-12 engine, the SL600 represents the ultimate in Mercedes-Benz sports cars in the 1990s. While the chassis in which the V-12 engine rides is no longer as light and sporty as the 300SL which began the line, the SL600 still represents the acme in luxury sports cars.

fourth-generation cars, summarized this approach thus: "Experience has shown that a car design which stands out against others by means of fancy avant-garde form elements is bound to be outdated quicker than those cars which deliberately shun such effects."

Bruno Sacco said that in his opinion the new cars, introduced in 1989, are the most attractive since the original 300SL. "In my opinion the most attractive Mercedes among the classic models is the 300SL convertible of 1957. In terms of more recent Mercedes it is the 500/600SL of 1989."

From the side, the R129 cars exhibit a distinct wedge shape. Modernized versions of the original 300SL's air scoops behind the front wheels were added.

The trapezoidal front light groupings were an integral part of the front fenders and help define the grille, which continued the tradition of the SL series but with modern design elements, such as anodized aluminum slats framing the integrated three-pointed star. Below the grille was a new bumper that incorporated invisible shock-absorbing elements. Taillights combined brake signals, turn signals, and backup lights in a shape that echoed the front lights. They incorporated the traditional Mercedes ribbed "dirt-free" design.

The cars' interior combined functionality and elegance, with an abundance of wood trim, leather, and easy-to-read instruments. Mercedes chose simple white-on-black instruments rather than the orange-light-bathed gauges favored by other manufacturers.

Front seat belts were mounted to the seats. All models had dual airbags to complement the belts. In later years, side-mounted airbags would be added.

In Europe, two 300SL variations were offered initially: the two-valve-per-cylinder 300SL and the four-valve-per-cylinder 300SL-24. The two-valve engine was rated at 190 hp, while the four-valve engine pumped out 231 horses. The larger 500SL was the most powerful SL for a while with a 5.0-liter V8 rated at 326 horsepower. In 1993 it was moved to second place when Mercedes introduced the 600SL with a 48-valve V12 engine rated at 389 horsepower.

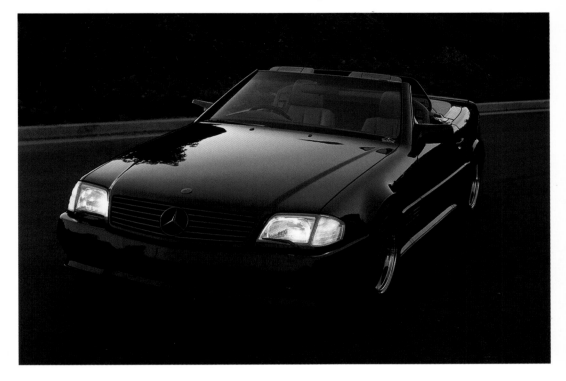

The V12 engine is impressive. It incorporates roller-chain-driven double overhead camshafts to actuate the valves, which are mounted at a 50-degree angle. A feature of the engine is the inlet camshaft adjustment, which improves the cylinders' volumetric efficiency depending on engine speed and torque demands.

With 315 hp, the 500SL V8 could propel the 3,894-pound car from 0–62 mph in 6.2 seconds. Top speed was an electronically limited 155 mph. When the 600SL was added to the line it, too, was limited to a maximum speed of 155 mph. Zero to 60 mph was 6.1 seconds, only marginally better than the 500SL. But the 600SL weighed nearly 600 pounds more (in the US) at 4,455 pounds.

In 1992, the renamed SL series was joined in Europe by the six-cylinder SL280, with a 193-DIN-hp engine. Performance was about the same as for the original R129 300SL. The new engine incorporated four-valves-per-cylinder technology with a variable intake manifold, an electrohydraulically adjustable intake camshaft and a microprocessor-controlled injection and ignition system that was designed to produce low emissions and high torque at low engine speeds. Both a five-speed manual and four-speed automatic transmission were offered.

Meanwhile, the 300SL was replaced by the SL320. This engine developed 228 SAE horsepower, the same as the 3.0-liter engine, but at a lower speed. This resulted in better fuel economy.

Above:
Mercedes-Benz dropped the SL320 in 1997 in favor of the SL500 and SL600. The SL500 received a new generation V-8 engine in 1999 that includes dual spark plus and three valves per cylinder. While it is a sophisticated engine, it still has the roar of a big V-8, rivaling the sound of some American sporty cars.

Chapter 7

The 1990s

The virtual explosion of new and varied models from Mercedes-Benz in the 1930s has been exceeded by the spate of new vehicles coming out of Sindlefingen and other factories around the world in the 1990s.

In 1992 an engineering study was conducted by Mercedes-Benz to decide the future direction of the company in various areas, among them the future of the G-Wagen. At its head was a young member of the management committee, Andreas Renschler.

In March 1992, Renschler, then 34, was appointed head of a project to decide if and where Mercedes-Benz should build a sport utility vehicle. By that time the sport utility market was in the middle of an explosion that would take it to US sales of more than 600,000 vehicles in a world market of more than 2 million vehicles by 1997. The luxury SUV segment at that time had maybe two competitors, the Land Rover and Jeep Grand Cherokee.

Renschler's training was in economic engineering and business administration. He had joined Mercedes-Benz in 1988 and was shortly a member of the staff of Helmut Werner, who would become the Chairman of the Board of Management.

The management board's goal was to steer Mercedes-Benz in new directions by the end of the century, not an easy charter in a 105-year-old company. Jürgen Hubbert, Mercedes-Benz board member for passenger cars, admitted that it would be difficult to accomplish. He said, "It is very difficult to turn around in such a short time. To do this you need three things: a vision, a strategy, and a very motivated team. The vision was clear. We said we wanted to be number one in profitability and innovation by the year 2000. We decided on four offensives: one for products, one for productivity, one for globalization, and one for learning."

Andreas Renschler and his team naturally looked at the possible redesign of the G-Wagen. But would a simple redesign of this slab-sided, expensive, boxy vehicle be consistent with Mercedes' goal of being number one in innovation? The answer was a resounding no.

Left:
In one of its most ambitious projects, Mercedes-Benz decided to produce the ML320 sport utility in the US. Not only was the vehicle a brand new entry for Mercedes, the Alabama factory was new and the management was multinational.

Right:
In creating the mid-size ML320, Mercedes-Benz designers used classic Mercedes design elements. The ML320 was unique in that its comportment off-road was as good as it was on-road.

The M-Class

According to the historian John Lamm, in *Mercedes-Benz M-Class*,

> If the company had stayed with the G-Wagen and given it a modern updating, the price would have come in at $55,000–60,000, with estimated sales of 5,000 per year in the US. By changing the aim of its sport-utility entry, Mercedes put the M-Class in the mid-$30,000 price range, which means sales may exceed 40,000 vehicles in the US alone. That price places the Mercedes-Benz SUV just above the fastest-growing portion of the sport-utility market. The result is that for a few extra dollars per month a buyer can move up from a Jeep Grand Cherokee or Ford Explorer to an M-Class, thus bringing new owners into the Mercedes fold. With some 25 percent of current US Mercedes-Benz owners already possessing a sport-utility vehicle, there was a built-in market for the M-Class. A higher-priced ($55,000–60,000) version of the G-Wagen would have had great appeal to traditional Mercedes-Benz buyers. But this new orientation of Mercedes' SUV says a great deal about the sorts of markets and customers the company wants to include in its future plans.

In October 1992, Renschler and his committee presented their basic plan to the management committee. Their suggestion was that Mercedes-Benz design and build a new sport utility vehicle, and that they build it in the United States. The plan was approved and followed by six months of frantic activity. In April 1993, Mercedes-Benz announced that it would build an all-new sport utility vehicle with the project name of AAV, or All Activity Vehicle. Mercedes also announced that they would build the vehicle in North America. Because Renschler had been so persuasive in his arguments, he was given the responsibility of heading the project.

Eventually, Mercedes-Benz created a new company, Mercedes-Benz United States International, with Andreas Renschler as president. Land was purchased and a factory erected in Vance, Alabama, on the outskirts of Tuscaloosa.

In the next three years, Mercedes displayed various concept cars under the name AAV at auto shows around the world. The vehicle that was shown was a rounded, swoopy vehicle in the classic SUV mode but also with classic Mercedes-Benz character. The vehicle was accompanied with predictions that the production AAV would offer excellent off-road capability, but would also ride and handle like a Mercedes-Benz automobile on the highway.

Mercedes-Benz celebrated the opening of its new factory in Alabama in May 1997. The first test vehicles rolled off the line and were an immediate success. When the M-Class was introduced to the media in Birmingham, Alabama, a month later it was a critical success. Initial production goals were 65,000 vehicles a year, with half designated for the US and the remainder for worldwide distribution. However, the initial popularity of the M-Class and its acclaim forced MBUSI to double production in 1997.

The M-Class not only was an all-new vehicle for Mercedes-Benz, but the company used it as the receptor for an all-new V6 engine, the first V6 in Mercedes-

Benz's history. This V6 was rated at 215 hp and worked through a five-speed automatic transmission. In addition, Mercedes-Benz incorporated all-wheel-drive technology, meaning that the driver did not have to worry about converting from two-wheel drive to four-wheel drive: the vehicle had sensors that determined which wheels needed the maximum traction and transferred power to those wheels. This permitted the driver to concentrate on driving, even if he or she was traversing the most rugged or slippery terrain.

To manufacture the M-Class in the most efficient manner, Mercedes suppliers also located factories in Alabama to reduce the time lost in transporting subsystems to Mercedes. Therefore, it is possible to have "Just In Time" (JIT) manufacturing, where only the exact number of dash assemblies, for example, for the next hour's production need be kept on hand. Mercedes-Benz factory personnel indicate that it is possible to order a number of assemblies from a manufacturer and have them on hand in under two

hours. These subsystem manufacturers in turn also practice JIT manufacturing, reducing their inventories to only what is necessary.

Besides its all-new factory, Mercedes-Benz also built a visitor center and museum at the Vance facility. This 20,000-square-foot museum contains many important vehicles in the company's history, including such early models as the Benz Patentmotorwagen, Daimler's motorcycle, early engines by the two, a Steinway American Mercedes, and a 300SL. The museum also houses an M-Class that appeared in the movie *The Lost World, Jurassic Park*, and the first M-Class to roll off the assembly line, signed by all the employees of MBUSI. Whilst it was not intended to be in quite the same league as the Mercedes-Benz Museum in Stuttgart, the American version of the Stuttgart facility gives visitors to the new factory, and those waiting to pick up their vehicles at the factory, an opportunity to get a taste of the company's enormous production and competition history.

Above (left and right)
Adapted from the All Activity Vehicle (AAV) concept vehicle, the ML320 had a modern dash with dash-mounted air bags for safety. Front passengers rode in leather-upholstered reclining seats with locking storage compartments underneath.

Right:

From the rear, the ML320 exhibits traditional sport utility lines, with the addition of a Mercedes-Benz three-pointed star. The ML320 will be sold throughout the world, with half its production slated for the US.

Far right:

Most sport utilities have poor road manners. The ML320, however, rides like a Mercedes-Benz sedan, giving the passengers a comfortable trip.

Right:

With 16-inch wheels, the ML320 has a larger footprint than the competition, giving the driver greater control.

Below:

In profile, there is no mistaking the ML320 for a sport utility. It is the only SUV with Mercedes-Benz on the skin and under the skin.

Model C112

Wheelbase (in.)	106.3
Overall length (in.)	122.0
Overall width (in.)	77.8
Overall height (in.)	47.0
Curb weight (lb.)	3460
Engine	6.0-liter v-12
Horsepower/Torque	408 @ 5200 rpm/ 430lb-ft @ 3800 rpm
Transmission	Six-speed

The C112 experimental car

Mercedes-Benz did not rest on the laurels of the C111 experimental car for very long. At the 1991 Frankfurt Auto Show the company showed the C112, which was the latest experimental car for the company. According to Karl Ludvigsen, "The C112 used materials, electronics, aerodynamics and advanced systems inspired by racing to give its driver unprecedented quality and confidence of control under all road conditions."

Bruno Sacco told *Auto & Design*, "When the C112 theme was being developed, we didn't get lost in the maze, tempted to be too trendy. It possesses a well-defined tradition, anchored in the past but coherently linked to design concepts developed over the last fifteen years. We tried to continue with what we retain as our design philosophy."

The C112 was a mid-engined design that was not at all unlike the Sauber-Mercedes Group C racers. But it also had bumpers, ABS, ASR (anti-wheelspin control, or traction control), tire-pressure monitoring and radar distance monitoring. In addition, the C112 used an active suspension system to keep the car level at all times. It was similar to the active suspensions used by Formula 1 racing teams.

The interior was luxuriously appointed as befitted a Mercedes-Benz, including a Blaupunkt Mexico 2000 AM/FM radio-cassette. The engine was a 6.0-liter V12 rated at 408 bhp and 430 pound-feet of torque.

Externally, the C112 resembled the cars it would have competed against: the Jaguar XJ220, Lamborghini Diablo, and Bugatti EB110. But the C112 was never placed into production or offered for sale, much like the C111.

Below:
After the C111 experimental car, Mercedes-Benz engineers did not rest on their laurels. Its successor was the C112, a super car with a 6.0-liter 408 bhp V-12 engine.

SL in the 1990s

The sporty SL series of cars – six-cylinder 300SL, eight-cylinder 500SL, and 12-cylinder 600SL – were by 1990 neither sporty nor light. While they were superb niche vehicles with outstanding engines and very good performance, they would never see the heat of competition on any race track. Mercedes' decision was to keep the SL cars (although the six-cylinder model was discontinued) and introduce a new small sports car, the SLK230, in 1996. (Mercedes-Benz had also, in 1993, changed the alphanumeric nomenclature of its cars. The 280C became the C280, for example, which indicated the class of car alphabetically and a three-digit number representing one-tenth of the engine's capacity in cc.) While still not as light as the original 300SL, the SLK230 was powered by a 2.3-liter, supercharged, inline, four-cylinder engine (the "K" in SLK stands for "Kompressor," or supercharger).

Above:
As the SL Class cars developed, they also moved out of the price range of many customers. In 1996, Mercedes-Benz moved to rectify this situation with the SLK230, a super-charged four-cylinder smaller sports car that offered exhilarating performance at a price under $40,000.

Left:
While it would be offered in Europe with a variety of engines, in the US the SLK would only have the 2.3-liter supercharged four.

SLK230

Wheelbase (in.)	94.5
Overall length (in.)	157.3
Overall width (in.)	67.5
Overall height (in.)	50.7
Curb weight (lb.)	3036
Engine	2.3-liter supercharged I-4
Horsepower	185 @ 5300 rpm
Transmission	Five-speed automatic
Fuel tank (gal.)	14.0

Above:
In attempting to lure a younger audience, Merecedes-Benz used striking colors and a dramatically styled interior in the SLK230.

Below:
What makes the SLK230 unique is its powered hard top, that automatically recesses into a compartment behind the rear seat.

Helmut Werner, president and CEO of Mercedes-Benz AG, said, "The small sports car is a milestone in the Mercedes-Benz passenger car product offensive, which began with the new E-Class and is reaching unprecedented intensity this year [1997]. The SLK is a car that honors in a particularly attractive way our company's claim to offer premium value, and it marks an aesthetic renaissance in automotive styling. More than this, with its lightness and flexibility, the SLK is in many ways symbolic of our company as a whole, which has become much faster-moving in recent years. But the development is not causing us to abandon our traditions. That, too, is abundantly evident from an examination of this car."

From the beginning, Mercedes-Benz deferred any comparison of the SLK230 to the mighty 300SL, preferring instead to associate it with the company's last four-cylinder sports car, the 190SL. This, of course, was a much more palatable comparison designed to put the SLK230 not only in a more favorable light but also in a more reasonable one.

The engine of the SLK230 is a 2.3-liter, double-overhead-cam, inline, four-cylinder equipped with a Roots-type supercharger. The basic engine, minus the supercharger, is also used in the C230 sedan, for example. It develops 191 horsepower at 5,300 rpm, nearly as much as the normally aspirated 2.8-liter six-cylinder engine used in the C280. Maximum torque is 206 lb/ft, slightly more than the C280.

Power reaches the road through an electronically controlled five-speed automatic transmission. The transmission adapts its shifting strategy in response to individual driving conditions and styles. It can "learn" to respond like a manual transmission operated by a skilled driver.

Front suspension is by double wishbones, while the rear suspension is a form of the patented five-link design that Mercedes-Benz has used since 1981. This design maintains tire contact under changing road conditions while providing the highest level of ride comfort. Gas-pressurized shock absorbers and coil springs are used at all four corners.

At its introduction, Mercedes-Benz estimated a 0–60 mph time of 7.2 seconds and a top speed of 143 mph for the SLK 230.

Despite its relatively compact size, the SLK offers the complete Mercedes-Benz safety arsenal. The SLK230 is equipped with Mercedes pioneering features, such as crumple-zone body construction, three-point seat belts, dual front airbags and knee bolsters, and anti-lock, four-wheel disc brakes. In addition, the SLK offers door-mounted side airbags for protection in the event of a side collision. Mercedes also pioneered the child safety seat, called BabySmart, which deactivates the front passenger-side airbag if a specially built child seat with sensors is used.

Rollover protection is offered by heavily reinforced sturdy A-pillars that retain their shape in a rollover situation, and fixed roll bars located behind the passenger seats. These roll bars are bolted to the top part of the rear bulkhead, which connects to the B-pillar stubs. They are covered in foam-plastic sheaths.

Above:
In 1993, Mercedes-Benz introduced a new C-Class sedan, called the W202, at the Frankfurt Auto Show. The compact C-Class would sell for under $30,000 in the US, and would become Mercedes-Benz's most popular car.

Below:
With trapezoidal headlights flanking a traditional Mercedes-Benz grille with pronounced horizontal bars, the new C-Class presents its own unique face to oncoming traffic.

C230	
Wheelbase (in.)	105.9
Overall length (in.)	177.4
Overall width (in.)	67.7
Overall height (in.)	56.1
Curb weight (lb.)	3250
Engine	2.3-liter I-4
Horsepower	148 @ 5500 rpm
Transmission	Five-speed automatic
Fuel tank (gal.)	16.4

The new C-Class

After a 10-year run during which they sold more than 1.9 million units, Mercedes-Benz introduced a new W202 C-Class at the 1993 Frankfurt Auto Show. Originally introduced as the 190 and 190E of 1982, those W201 cars were extensively reworked versions of the larger 200 series that once again established Mercedes-Benz as builders of compact sedans.

C-Class (C is for "Compact", although in German it's "Kompaktklasse") cars were powered by a variety of four- and six-cylinder engines using gasoline and diesel fuels. Dimensionally, they were slightly larger than the cars they replaced – wheelbase increased by 1.0 inch to 105.9 inches; overall length by 3.4 inches to 177.4 inches; width by 1.7 inches to 67.7 inches; height by 1.3 inches to 55.7 inches; and weight by 594 pounds to 2,970 pounds – the new cars were also rounder and more aerodynamic. With the increased size came improved interior dimensions as well. An improved front suspension made for better handling and ride characteristics.

The front suspension consisted of upper and lower control arms, coil springs and a stabilizer bar with antidive geometry and negative offset steering. In the back was the Mercedes-Benz multilink design with coil springs, a stabilizer bar and antilift and antisquat geometry. Antilift keeps the front tires in better contact with the road under hard acceleration; antisquat keeps the car level under heavy braking.

The new 1.8-liter four-cylinder engine in the base C180 incorporated double overhead camshafts and four-valves-per-cylinder technology to deliver 122 DIN horsepower. It was the most popular of the new C-Class models, even though it was not available in the United States. Next up the size line was the C200 with a 2.0-liter four that was a bored-out version of the 180. The 1.8-liter's bore and stroke were 85.3 x 78.7 mm (3.35 x 3.10 in.), while the 2.0's were 89.9 x 78.7 mm (3.54 x 3.10 in). The 2.2-liter of the C220 was the 200's engine but with a longer stroke (86.6 mm or 3.41 in.). The C220 was the only four-cylinder available in the United States and was rated at 147 SAE hp. In 1993, it sold for $29,900 in the US, the only Mercedes-Benz under $30,000. It was also the most popular American model.

The six-cylinder C-Class engine was the 2.8-liter unit rated at 194 SAE hp. Good performance was available from the C280, with a 0–60 mph time of 8.4 seconds and a top speed of more than 140 mph.

Diesel-engined models included a 2.0, 2.2, and 2.5-liter model. None were available in the United States. The C200 offered 75 DIN hp; the 220, 95 DIN hp; the 250, 113 DIN hp.

The relationship with AMG

For years, Mercedes-Benz has had a close working relationship with the AMG company. AMG stands for the names of the two principals of the company, Hans Werner Aufrecht and Erhard Melcher and their location, Grossapach. The relationship has led to the development of a group of competition sedans that has created virtual ownership of the European Touring Car championship for Mercedes.

Collaboration on the race track led to collaboration on the sales floor. In 1994, Mercedes-Benz introduced the C36, which was a C280 "tweaked" by AMG. Where the C280 had a 2.8-liter 24-valve DOHC six-cylinder engine that delivered 194 SAE hp, the C36 used a six-cylinder version of the engine that displaced 3.6 liters and was rated at 268 SAE hp. The extra capacity was arrived at by enlarging the bore and lengthening the stroke. AMG increased the compression from 10.5:1 to 10.0:1.

In addition, AMG installed a five-speed manual or four-speed automatic transmission from the V8-engined E420 and E500, added larger front disc brakes from the SL600 and rear brakes from the E420. Seventeen-inch wheels filled the wheel arches with 225/45ZR tires in front and 225/40ZR tires in the rear.

Acceleration from 0–62 mph was nearly two seconds quicker than with the stock C280 at 6.9 seconds. Top speed was a limited 156 mph, compared with 144 mph for the C280.

AMG also added a front air dam, lower side body cladding that kept "dirty air" from under the car, and special interior and exterior markings.

In 1998, Mercedes-Benz introduced the next generation AMG car, a C43AMG. With a 4.3-liter V8 engine, it is the first V8-powered C-Class sedan. Making use of three-valves-per-cylinder technology, the engine develops 305 DIN hp, compared with 278 for the standard engine. With a standard five-speed automatic transmission, the C43AMG can accelerate to 62 mph in 6.5 seconds. Top speed is 155 mph.

Among the engine changes are camshafts with individually forged lobes that are placed on the tubes. Intake and exhaust cams were designed for longer valve opening times, increasing power. The engine also used a double-fluted intake system and larger intake manifold.

Underneath, the C43AMG used a C-Class sports suspension that lowered the body by one inch and included reinforced torsion bars and stiffer gas shock absorbers. The safety system known as ESP (Electronic Stability Program) is also standard in the C43AMG (see following page).

The new E-Class

While the C-Class sedans soldiered along as Mercedes-Benz's most profitable and popular sedans and coupes, the company introduced a new E-Class in 1995. Where the C-Class, previous E-Class, and S-Class presented the classic Mercedes-Benz "face" to oncoming cars of vertical honeycomb grille surrounded by rectangular headlights, the new E-Class (E is for "Executive" class or "Mittelereklasse" (middle class)) used oval-shaped headlights and a sloping (albeit, still honeycomb) grille. This more aerodynamic approach set the E-Class apart, not only from its siblings at Mercedes, but from almost all other manufacturers, whose designs were tending more and more toward rectangular lights or shaped lights incorporating halogen beams.

Above:
Mercedes-Benz's "Executive" or "Mittelerklasse" sedan is the E-Class, introduced in 1995. What sets the E-Class sedans and E320 wagon apart are the oval headlights and running lights. Notice, too, the trend toward a grille with pronounced horizontal bars, rather than a crosshatching as in earlier cars.

As with all Mercedes models, under the hood of the E-Class there could be any one of a variety of Mercedes-Benz engines, from a 2.3-liter four-cylinder to a 4.2-liter V8 or a 3.0-liter turbodiesel. In the United States, the most popular model was the E320, with the 3.2-liter V6 developed for the M-Class.

Electronic Stability Program (ESP)

In 1996, Mercedes-Benz introduced its Electronic Stability Program, which works to help keep the car going in the direction the driver points it. Initially offered as standard equipment on the company's V12-powered models, it soon became available on all the company's sedans, coupes, and roadsters.

Mike Jackson, Mercedes-Benz of North America president, said ESP was a technology breakthrough that should help reduce accidents. "We think it could prove to be the most significant accident-avoidance development since anti-lock brakes," Jackson said.

ESP uses electronic sensors and computer logic to calculate every one thousandth of a second if the car is

E320	
Wheelbase (in.)	111.5
Overall length (in.)	189.4
Overall width (in.)	70.8
Overall height (in.)	56.7
Curb weight (lb.)	3460
Engine	3.2-liter V-6
Horsepower	221 hp @ 5500 rpm
Transmission	Five-speed automatic
Fuel tank (gal.)	21.1

going in the direction it is being steered. If there is any difference between what the driver is asking through the steering wheel and what the vehicle is doing, the system corrects with split-second speed by applying one of the left- or right-side brakes, even before the driver may sense any changes.

The system uses the angle of the steering wheel and the speed of the four tires to calculate the path being steered. It uses electronic signals about lateral Gs and vehicle yaw to measure what the car is actually doing. It

measures any tendency toward understeer (when a car is slow to respond to steering changes) or oversteer (when the rear wheels try to swing around). If it senses understeer in a turn, ESP increases brake pressure to the inside rear wheel. With oversteer, it increases brake pressure to the outside front wheel.

The CLK

In 1996 Mercedes debuted the CLK coupe with a 3.2-liter V6, calling it the CLK320. As part of a new coupe strategy that differentiates coupes from the base sedans, the CLK resembles the E-Class from the front with its distinctive use of oval headlights. In reality, though, the CLK and E-Class share no body panels, and the "face" of the CLK is of slightly smaller proportions. While the CLK is the smaller of the two coupe families, the CL series of coupes is derived from the S-Class coupes and

they are much larger (K in this case is for "Kurtz", or "short"). The CLK shares a number of C-Class and SLK underbody components. It has a content level similar to the E-Class, but has a unique interior design.

Mercedes-Benz displayed a Geneva Coupe Concept at the 1993 Geneva Auto Salon that previewed the front-end treatment of both the E-Class and the CLK.

With a 61-degree slope to the windshield and a

Above:
Introduced in 1996, the CLK Coupe is built on the C-Class platform and offers aerodynamic fastback styling. Like all Mercedes-Benz vehicles, the CLK320, with a 3.2-liter V-6, has a full luxury interior.

Left:
Even though it shares a platform with the C-Class, the CLK320 Coupe has an "E-Class" front fascia, albeit slightly smaller.

CLK320

Wheelbase (in.)	105.9
Overall length (in.)	180.2
Overall width (in.)	67.8
Overall height (in.)	53.0
Curb weight (lb.)	3240
Engine	3.20 liter V-6
Horsepower	215 hp @ 5500 rpm
Transmission	Five-speed automatic
Fuel tank (gal.)	16.4

more sweeping roofline than previous Mercedes-Benz coupes, the CLK is more aerodynamic than its predecessors. The coefficient of drag is a low 0.30, thanks in part to the designed-in details that direct airflow around the body.

Unlike most coupes, it has true seating for four adults. In addition, there is an Easy Entry System that makes it easier for rear-seat passengers to enter and exit the car. The system uses the power-seat mechanism to quickly move the front seats forward, and then return them to their preset position.

The front passenger seat features an occupant sensor, which detects the presence of a person sitting in the passenger seat. Should the system detect nothing in the passenger seat, the passenger-side front and side airbags do not deploy, saving considerable repair cost. Rear seat belts automatically adjust for passenger height, ensuring comfort for a variety of physiques.

Expanding the model proliferation in 1998, Mercedes debuted the CLK Cabriolet at the Geneva Motor show in March. The CLK320 Cabriolet and more powerful V8-powered CLK430 Coupe were the latest developments in the company's product explosion of the 1990s.

The CLK stands alongside the SL and SLK roadsters as a fun-to-drive, open-air car with ample seating for four. With a fully lined and insulated top, the CLK Cabriolet also has a glass rear window with electric defroster for maximum visibility. The storage compartment for the top and its mechanism are part of the trunk, reducing trunk capacity by approximately 60 percent when the top is down.

Cross members in the Cabriolet's floor are reinforced to ensure body rigidity. The A-pillars and windshield frame are specially designed to increase protection in the event of a rollover. The rear head restraints, which usually protrude only slightly above the rear deck, pop up automatically if the car senses an impending rollover.

Among the technical innovations offered by Mercedes-Benz in 1998 is SmartKey, a unique electronic key fob that replaces the standard metal ignition key. The fob contains a radio frequency unit to

Left:
Joining the CLK320 Coupe in 1998 are the CLK320 Cabriolet, and the V-8-powered CLK430 Coupe that offers more power.

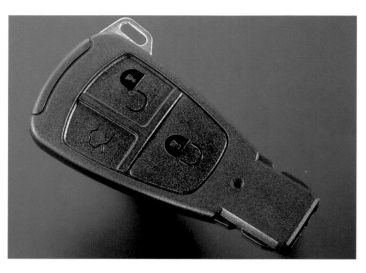

lock and unlock the doors and a separate system to start the car. The driver inserts the pointed tip of the fob into the "key" slot and turns it. An infrared data exchange between the car and the remote unit unlocks the steering column and engages the starter motor. For maximum security, the code needed to unlock and start the car are changed each time the car is used.

The S-Class

The ultimate Mercedes-Benz luxury car is the S-Class (S for "Sonderklasse" or "Super"), offered in standard (119.7 inches) and extended (123.6 inches) wheelbase versions. The various entries in that class are the S320, with a 228-horsepower, 3.2-liter, V6 engine; S420 with a 275-hp, 4.2-liter V8; S500, with a 315-hp, 5.0-liter V8; and the ultimate S600 with a 389-hp 6.0-liter V12. All engines transmit their power to the rear wheels through electronically controlled five-speed automatic transmissions that adapt to an individual's driving style as well as to changes in road grade.

Among the standard luxury features on the S-Class are full leather upholstery, 12-way power front seats, eucalyptus or burl walnut wood trim, velour floor carpeting and floor mats, and an 11-speaker Bose sound system. But the S-Class also offers unique pneumatic door and trunk closing assist to prevent "door ajar" situations. These assists pull the doors and trunk closed the last few inches of their travel.

For comfort, there is a dual-zone automatic climate-control system that features dust and pollen filters. In cold weather there is a mode to recirculate warm air for up to 30 minutes when the car is parked. On the S600 there are separate rear dual-zone climate controls. A rain sensor detects rainfall on the windshield and, using infrared technology, measures rainfall intensity and adjusts wiper speed accordingly.

Making parking easier and safer is the optional Parktronic system, which acts like sonar to warn the driver of obstacles when driving. Sensors built into the front and rear bumpers emit ultrasonic signals, which bounce off obstacles such as parked cars, curbs, shrubs and even children, and activate audible and visual warnings inside the car.

The S-Class sedans were originally shown for the first time in Frankfurt in 1985, and were only slightly "retouched" over the following 13 years.

Above:
Many Grand Prix drivers have selected the S500 coupe as their personal car. It offers luxury, performance, and traditional Mercedes-Benz reliability.

S600	
Wheelbase (in.)	123.6
Overall length (in.)	205.2
Overall width (in.)	74.3
Overall height (in.)	58.3
Curb weight (lb.)	4960
Engine	6.0-liter V-12
Horsepower	389 hp @ 5600 rpm
Transmission	Five-speed automatic
Fuel tank (gal.)	26.4

S500

Wheelbase (in.)	123.6
Overall length (in.)	205.2
Overall width (in.)	74.3
Overall height (in.)	58.5
Curb weight (lb.)	4700
Engine	5.0-liter V-8
Horsepower	315 hp @ 5600 rpm
Transmission	Five-speed automatic
Fuel tank (gal.)	26.4

Right:
With the 6.0-liter V-12, the 1998 S600 sedan is Mercedes-Benz's most luxurious and expensive car, at $135,000.

Competition

Right:
Mercedes-Benz entered this CLK-GTR racer in selected sports car events. While not as aerodynamic as many prototype sports cars because of its "E-Type" front fascia, it was still a formidable car.

Formula 1

Mercedes-Benz's withdrawal from the World Sports Car Championship at the end of 1991 should have signaled an end to high-level competition efforts from the company. After all, Werner Niefer had said, "In the future the Mercedes-Benz AG will concentrate its motor-sports activities on the support of capable touring-car teams, [and] will no longer take part in Group D and will not enter Formula 1."

But while the company was committed not to compete in 1992, pressure was building toward the end of 1991 for Mercedes-Benz to enter Formula 1 racing in 1992 in support of the Sauber team. For his part, Sauber had built a new dedicated facility with 70,000 square feet of working area, hired a staff of 70, signed the drivers Michael Schumacher and Karl Wendlinger, and recruited the experienced Formula 1 designer Harvey Postlethwaite to his team. Sauber also contracted with Mario Illien and Paul Morgan of Ilmor to design an engine for his car.

Below:
Sauber campaigned for Mercedes at Le Mans with this C9 racer. With a relatively small team, Sauber won the 24-hour race twice.

Sauber built the racers with 30 million Deutschmarks from Mercedes-Benz as support. An additional DM30 million was sought for sponsorship. But, despite the fact that Goodyear recognized the value of the Sauber-Mercedes association, no further sponsorship was forthcoming. Sauber competed through the 1993 season solely on the Mercedes-Benz money.

The engine chosen for the Sauber car was a V10 design of Ilmor's that would deliver 670 hp at 12,800 rpm. Wendlinger and J.J. Lehto were the team's drivers, since Schumacher's talent had already been recognized and he had joined the Bennetton team. While neither driver achieved a podium finish during the 1993 season, each had reached as high as fourth and the team finished sixth in the constructor's championship, tied with Lotus.

For 1994, Mercedes-Benz announced it would compete in Formula 4, Indy cars, and the German Touring Car championship. In addition, the traditional silver cars had to give way to cars whose class represented sponsorship dollars.

Right:
In Formula 1, Mercedes supplies engines to the McLaren team. In the first races of the 1998 season, drivers Mika Hakkinen and David Coulthard dominated the series with four one-two finishes.

In October 1993, Mercedes announced that it would back motorsports in three areas: Formula 1, Indy Car and touring cars. In fact, although the engines would carry Mercedes-Benz identification, they were Ilmor designs that were not based on any current Mercedes-Benz production engines. Still, the slogan "Concept by Mercedes-Benz" on the Sauber cars was soon to be joined by "Powered by Mercedes-Benz" on the Roger Penske Indy car team.

For Sauber, 1994 was disappointing. Wendlinger was seriously injured at Monte Carlo and the best finish by any Sauber driver was a sixth place by Heinz-Harald Frentzen at Spain. The team finished eighth in the team standings.

The season was disappointing on another note. Mercedes-Benz chose to remove its support from Sauber after the 1994 season, particularly since Sauber was unable to attract additional sponsorship. For the 1995 season, Mercedes-Benz engines would power McLaren racers. Drivers were Mika Hakkinen, the former World Champion Nigel Mansell, and Martin

Below:
Mercedes-Benz re-entered Formula 1 in 1994 with the Sauber team that had helped it to two World Sports Car Championships. The Sauber effort was not as successful as Mercedes would have hoped for and the company switched its support to McLaren following the 1994 season.

Blundell. Schumacher became freed of his Bennetton contract at the end of the 1996 season and the McLaren team manager Ron Dennis was anxious to sign the brilliant German. The feelings were mutual. "To become world champion with Mercedes – that would be the greatest," Schumacher said. "Because the

history that was written by the Silver Arrows goes right to the heart. If one could be linked again to this tradition it would be fantastic."

Unfortunately for Mercedes, Schumacher's desire for a contract that would allegedly offer him in excess of $20 million a year was beyond what McLaren-Mercedes was willing to pay him and he signed with Ferrari for 1997 and 1998.

While it took two years for the team's efforts to come together, Hakkinen won the final grand prix race of the 1997 season and was dominant in the early races of the 1998 season.

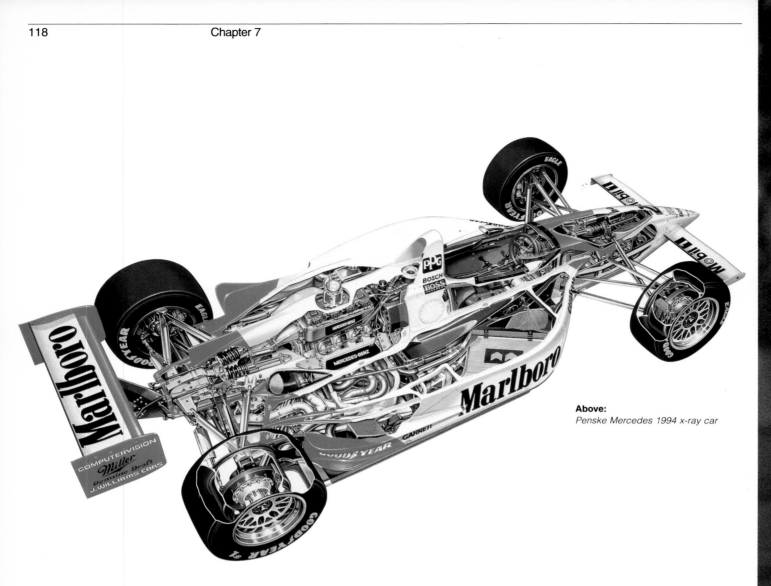

Above:
Penske Mercedes 1994 x-ray car

Indianapolis

Mercedes also is a supplier of engines to the Championship Auto Racing Teams (CART) series of Indianapolis-style racing in the United States. With Ilmor Engineering's experience in building Chevrolet engines for the series, and the fact that 50 percent of Ilmor was owned by Roger Penske, who is the car owner with the most Indy Car wins in history, there was a connection.

The series had been dominated by Offenhauser engines through the 1940s and 1950s. When Jimmy Clark won the Indianapolis 500 in 1965 it ushered in the era of the Ford Cosworth. Ford won the Indy 500 six times, was replaced by the Offy for five years, then came back (as the Cosworth) to dominate the race until 1988, when Rick Mears won with a Chevy Indy V8, an engine developed and built by Ilmor. Buick, Honda, and Toyota had also tried to build engines for the most famous race in the world, but with little success.

Ilmor's contract with Chevrolet expired at the end of the 1993 season. After several months of negotiation, the company contracted with Mercedes-Benz to develop a new generation of Indy Car engines that would wear the Mercedes-Benz name. The engines were built to a 2,650-cc capacity, turbocharged with overhead camshafts. The engines would develop in the neighborhood of 940 horsepower.

Mercedes-Benz committed to become a participant in the engine Ilmor was designing for the 1994 Indianapolis 500 in October 1993 when it acquired a 20-percent stake in Ilmor's Detroit subsidiary, then purchased 25 percent of Ilmor UK, a move which effectively bought out GM.

The first Ilmor Mercedes-Benz Indy Car engine ran on a dynamometer in England and developed 965 to 970 hp and 557 lb/ft of torque. In qualifying, Al Unser Jr qualified on the pole at a speed of 228.011 mph for four laps, 10 miles. Emerson Fittipaldi was third fastest at 227.303 mph.

In the race, Fittipaldi led for 145 laps until he made a mental mistake that put his car into the wall. Al Unser Jr. inherited the lead on lap 184 and held it to the finish. His average speed for the 500 miles was 160.872 mph.

The Ilmor Mercedes-Benz engine was to have been used for the 1995 Indy Car season. Unfortunately, the United States Auto Club reduced the allowable boost of the engine by almost 13 percent, making it uncompetitive. Therefore, the engine ran only one race, but proved to be imminently successful in that race.

Penske Racing and several other CART Indy Car teams have used Mercedes-Benz engines in competition since that time, although not the 500I engine developed for that one race. Penske dominated the series in 1994, but received renewed competition from Honda in 1995, during which season Honda won the championship. Honda was dominant in 1996 and 1997 with the Chip Ganassi team. In the early races of the 1998 season, however, it has been the Ford Cosworth that has won, making for a well-balanced championship and the prospect of an exciting conclusion to the year.

Above:
Mercedes also competes in the CART Champ Car series with the Penske-Marlboro team. The 1994 Penske Mercedes car won the Indianapolis 500 that year.

Chapter 8

New Directions

Mercedes-Benz introduced two new vehicles in the late 1990s that were complete departures from the company's core business of big luxurious cars. These were the A-Class and the Smart Car, built in a joint venture with the Swiss watchmaker Swatch.

The A-Class, while being Mercedes-Benz's first small car, is also one of the safest, with innovative technology designed into the car to protect the occupants. For example, the car makes use of a concept called the "sandwich principle," which provides a floor for the interior of the car that is separated from the bottom floor pan of the vehicle.

The floor is totally flat from the driver's footwell all the way back to the rear bumper. The fuel tank, suspension, and battery are all stored below deck, along with other mechanical parts. The engine and transmission of the front-wheel-drive A-Class are tilted, reducing wasted space.

In a frontal impact, the angled engine and transmission block slide under the body, rather than punching into the passenger compartment. This also means that the crumple zone – the deformable part of the front of the car that absorbs impact – is entirely dedicated to the task of progressive deformation. To ensure this, a special integral subframe is used so that in the event of a serious crash, the engine and transmission are released, allowing them to pass beneath the vehicle.

Crash tests against larger vehicles and deformable barriers indicate that occupants are not at a substantial disadvantage, which is what you would expect from a car that is just 141.8 inches long. In the event of a side-impact collision, passengers are effectively sitting above the crash zone and are protected from it because they are eight inches higher than they would be in a conventional car.

Four engines are planned for the A-Class: a 1,397-cc, 82-hp gasoline engine in the A140; a 1,598-cc, 102-hp gasoline engine for the A160; a 1,689-cc, 60-hp turbodiesel for the A160 Turbodiesel; and a 90-hp version of the 1,689-cc engine for the A170 Turbodiesel. If the vehicle is ever exported to the United States, it may be with an electric motor

Left:
In 1998, Mercedes-Benz entered an entirely new arena with the subcompact A-Class, developed from this prototype. While it is tiny on the outside, the A-Class offers exceptional interior space and remarkable safety for a car of its size.

powering it, and not until early in the next century.

The A-Class offers the space of a family sedan in the space of a mini car. The generous glass area complements the A-Class's spacious interior, with the rear windows, which wrap around to the C-pillar, adding light to the interior. There is a wing-shaped instrument panel that seems to float beneath the windshield. In the exterior, the classic Mercedes grille was reinterpreted for the A-class, with teardrop-shaped headlights tying together the fenders, hood, and front bumper into an integrated package.

Despite extensive testing by Mercedes-Benz, the best laid schemes, as they say, often go astray. In testing in Finland in late 1997, the A-Class tipped over and flunked an "elk test."

As a tribute to Daimler-Benz, the company recalled all the 2,600 or so vehicles that had been delivered up to the time of notification and loaned the owners another Mercedes-Benz while their cars were being retrofitted. At a cost to the company of 100 million Deutschmarks, the chassis suspension of the A-Class was redesigned, with new stabilizer tunings on the front and rear axles, lowering of the body, and tires with new dimensions. In addition, the A-Class was fitted with the Electronic Stability Program.

"We take both the publicly expressed criticism and, in particular, the worries of our customers extremely

Left:
The A-Class initially "failed" the infamous Finnish "moose test," which is an avoidance maneuver. After recalling all the production cars to that time, Mercedes-Benz redesigned the A-Class, making it more stable in sudden avoidance maneuvers.

Below:
With concern about the danger to infants from air bags, Mercedes-Benz developed this BabySmart seat that detects the presence of an infant seat in the front seat of an SLK230 and turns off the passenger-side air bag.

seriously," said Jürgen E. Schrempp, Chairman of the Board of Management of Daimler-Benz AG. "That the A-Class has shown a weakness in extreme test situations is something nobody regrets more than we do. Our engineers have devoted all their energy, day and night, to the search for the optimal solution."

Besides the cost of developing a solution to this unexpected problem, Daimler-Benz estimated that there would be a negative impact of 100 million Deutschmarks in 1997 and a negative impact of 200 million Deutschmarks in 1998 because of the conversion and loss of sales.

These losses were mitigated by the respect Mercedes-Benz gained by its handling of the situation.

The Smart

Mercedes-Benz's other small car is the Smart, a sporty little two-seater that is built by a joint venture company established between Mercedes-Benz and the Swatch in 1994. Production of the Smart was initially scheduled for late 1997 with cars expected to reach dealers by the spring of 1998, but there was a snag. The Smart, like the larger A-Class, flunked a so-called "elk test," and had to be withheld for additional design changes. (The elk test is a special test the Finnish government conducts to see if a vehicle can avoid a large animal that might be standing in the middle of the road. The vehicle is accelerated to the test speed, which is under 50 mph, and the driver swerves right to avoid the "animal" and then left to get back onto the path he or she was following.)

Smart is trendsetting in many different ways. It is specifically optimized for city environments and responds to mobility demands with maximum driving pleasure, comfort, safety, technical refinement, and environmental compatibility.

With city traffic usually having 1.2 persons per private car, Smart was designed as a two-seater. Supercompact overall dimensions make parking easier and save money because of low fuel consumption. The Smart is only 2.5 meters long (98 inches) and could park perpendicular to the curb if local legislation permitted it.

The Smart will be made in Germany, Switzerland, and France: motors will come from Germany, electronics from Switzerland, and the end product will be assembled at the Micro Compact Car Company plant in Hambach, France.

One Mercedes-Benz board member, Jürgen Hubbert, said the Smart would go on sale at a price of $9,350 to $11,600. There are no plans, however, to sell it outside Europe.

In mid-1998 the Micro Compact Car Company unveiled new plans for as many as a half dozen sales outlets in Europe. Initial reaction to the announcement was favorable.

The Future

In a fitting tribute to one of the founders of Daimler-Motoren-Gesellschaft AG, Mercedes-Benz introduced the Maybach Design Study at the 1998 North American International Auto Show in Detroit. But more than just a tribute to Wilhelm Maybach, the Maybach Design Study showcased technology and features that the carmaker might include in a luxury car of the future. Needless to say, it is an automobile that could be built by Mercedes-Benz.

Mercedes-Benz positioned the Maybach Design Study in what it calls the "ultimate luxury" class of automobiles. This class would be above the current S-Class range of sedans, which is among the leaders in terms of technology, room, and features.

Of course, the Maybach Design Study honors Wilhelm Maybach, who was instrumental in the design of Daimler's first gasoline engine. After leaving Daimler-Benz he started his own car company, which specialized in large, elegant luxury models, the most famous of which was the 12-cylinder Maybach Zeppelin of the 1930s. Maybach Motoren GmbH joined the Daimler-Benz group in 1961.

The Maybach Design Study is powered by a V12 engine of just under six liters in displacement. It shares the innovative three-valve, twin-spark technology of the Mercedes-Benz V6 for efficiency and low emissions. The engine develops in excess of 400 horsepower.

Maybach Motoren GmbH specialized in building large automobiles, and the Maybach Design Study is a large car. It is 227.2 inches long from bumper to bumper, 22 inches longer than the Mercedes S-Class sedans. Still, the Maybach is shorter than most conventional limousines, but only four inches longer than a Lincoln Town Car. The Maybach is 61 inches tall, compared with 58.6 inches for the S-Class, and it is 2.4 inches wider than an S-Class at 76.8 inches. All this is built on a 139.4-inch wheelbase, nearly 15 inches longer than a Bentley Turbo RT.

There is more to the Maybach than simply size. Mercedes-Benz chose this venue to provide the ultimate luxury experience for passengers. The interior offers sumptuous seating and trim and the possibility of build-to-order custom equipment. Passengers will be able to control ambient light inside the vehicle. The unique glass roof allows passengers to control how much light enters the car and automatically regulates the amount of heat entering the car. Beneath the glass is a transparent layer of conductive polymer. The amount of light it allows to pass is controlled by applying voltage to it. An additional electrochromatic layer reacts to the level of ultraviolet rays entering the car to control interior heat build-up.

Rear-seat passengers are treated to electrically adjustable reclining seats. Each seat functions like a home reclining chair, with swivel-out supports for the lower legs. The right-side seat features an integral footrest, while in front of the left-side seat, in the floor, is a storage area for a pair of shoes. The top of this space serves as another footrest.

Also included in the Maybach is an onboard bar for serving hot and cold drinks. Located between the front seats, the bar features three different temperature-controlled serving areas. In addition, a "cool box" located under a folding armrest in the rear can accommodate a bottle of wine or champagne. For cigar aficionados, there is a humidor made of walnut and root wood between the rear seats.

For the business executive, the Maybach can serve as an office on wheels. For convenience, there are fold-down tables located under the armrests of the rear doors. The integrated communications and audio system features three telephones: a hands-free system for the driver, a second cordless telephone for the rear passengers, and a dedicated data line for sending e-mail and faxes. There is a portable computer in the glove box, which communicates using infrared technology, eliminating the need for cables.

For entertainment, there is a thin-profile 20-inch LCD screen that is just two inches deep suspended from the roof between the driver and front passenger. Passengers can use it to view television programs, DVD video, and VCR tapes, or play computer games.

The Maybach is equipped with a CD changer and a minidisc system. Rear-seat passengers can control all

Above:
Mercedes-Benz exhibited the Maybach concept car at auto shows, throughout 1998, with a V-12 engine and luxuries to make any potentate drool. At the publication date of this book, no decision had been made on whether the Maybach will be produced, but if it is, the probable price will be in the $300,000 range.

audio, video, and communication functions using six-inch touch-sensitive screens mounted on the B-pillars.

In the trunk of the Maybach is the ultimate luxury: two color-coded golf bags with a full set of professional-caliber clubs.

The Maybach driver is provided with an advanced instrument panel that conveys all the information desired by the driver. The panel is divided into normal instrument functions such as speedometer, odometer, fuel-level and temperature gauges, a field for warning messages and current weather and traffic conditions, and another screen that displays the view to the rear for safety, provided by a video camera.

Mercedes-Benz has equipped the Maybach with the latest in safety equipment, starting with the headlights,

which are unlike any others in production. These lights automatically change intensity, adapting to road and weather conditions. Taillight intensity also adjusts to ambient lighting conditions.

The Maybach also incorporates Brake Assist, which can detect a panic stop and apply full brake force automatically, more quickly than the driver can. When Brake Assist is engaged, the brake lights glow with more intensity to alert drivers following of an emergency condition ahead.

For the best ride quality, the Maybach Design Concept incorporates an Active Body Control chassis. Instead of springs at each wheel, there are hydraulic cylinders that generate counterforces in response to wheel load.

The Merger with Chrysler

On May 6, 1998, the automotive and business world awoke to shocking news; Daimler-Benz AG and Chrysler Corporation would merge in a $39.5 billion transaction that would create the world's fifth largest automobile manufacturer, behind General Motors, Ford, Toyota and Volkswagen. The announcement was made official a day later in Stuttgart in a joint press conference with Jürgen Schrempp of Daimler and Robert Eaton of Chrysler.

According to The Wall Street Journal, "Combined, the new company would be a $130 billion colossus with more than 420,000 employees; the two companies sold about four million vehicles (in 1997), from Chrysler's minivans and Jeep sport-utility vehicles to Daimler's luxury Mercedes sedans.

"Under the deal, a new company incorporated in Germany would be created to merge Chrysler and Daimler, though there would still be 'operational headquarters' in both Stuttgart, Germany, and Auburn Hills, Michigan. Each firm would receive five board seats in the new megacompany, and labor would receive an additional 10 seats, as required under German law. Mr. Schrempp and Mr. Eaton would hold co-chief executive positions for three years after the merger is completed; how a successor CEO would be chosen isn't yet clear."

The world's biggest corporate merger to that time began with a simple conversation between the two chairmen on January 12, 1998, at Chrysler's headquarters in Auburn Hills. Schrempp had called on Eaton while he was attending the Detroit Auto Show. He suggested that the two companies merge.

"I'd been thinking about the same thing," Eaton responded. Two weeks later, Eaton told Schrempp, "I would be interested in pursuing it." Eaton notified the Chrysler Board of Directors on February 5, after which Eaton and Chrysler Chief Financial Officer Gary Valade flew to Europe for a meeting with Daimler.

In order to keep the proposed merger a secret until all the details could be ironed out, code names were used for each of the companies. Chrysler was "Cleveland" and Daimler was "Denver."

Right:
One interesting aspect of the merged DaimlerChrysler is the fact that Jeep Grand Cherokees and Mercedes-Benz ML320s will be competing for the same customers.

According to Eaton, the name of the conglomerate was the final issue addressed. "It was a very emotional issue at the end, emotional on both sides," Schrempp said. "We both felt strongly."

Chrysler wanted "Chrysler Daimler-Benz." Daimler-Benz wanted "Daimler-Benz Chrysler." On May 5, they agreed on DaimlerChrysler. "It looked great and had a lot of class to it," Eaton said.

The merged company faces myriad obstacles to success, not the least of which is that as a German-based company it may lose the import-free shipping of cars to Canada. One primary advantage to the merger is that both companies use CATIA engineering software.

Daimler brings premium engineering know-how and high technology to the table; Chrysler is excellent in manufacturing, particularly low-cost manufacturing, according to Schrempp. Quality has always been a problem for Chrysler, while the company has been innovative in bringing new products to the marketplace in a short period of time. Chrysler's strengths are its low-cost four-cylinder engines and its ability to bring low-cost vehicles to market. Daimler's strengths are its direct-injection diesel engines and its fuel cell research, combined with an excellent reputation for quality.

Three weeks prior to the announced merger, Mercedes-Benz of North America put its plans for a new headquarters on hold. MBNA had planned to move its headquarters from Montvale, New Jersey, to Pearl River, New York, approximately 10 miles away.

The official announcement cited spiraling costs that threatened the $50 million cap on the design study and building. A Mercedes-Benz spokesman said later, "Now you know why we put a hold on the building."

Mercedes-Benz obviously hasn't stood still, even though it is an "old" company with roots that go back more than 115 years. Unlike humans of the same age, though, Mercedes-Benz appears to be enjoying a second childhood, with exciting new products, new ventures and new directions that can only lead to a continuance of the dominance of the three-pointed star (will it be eight points with the addition of Chrysler?) in the firmament of automotive history and current events.

Index

Adler, Denis 63
Aircraft engines 25, 43
Alfa Romeo 39,51
Alfieri, Bruno 92
AMG 81,104
Aston Martin DB2 51
Aufrecht, Hans Werner 105
Automobile Club of France 19

BMC 19
Barbarou, Marius 17
Barémyi, Béla 47
Bauer, Wilhelm 18
Benz, Bertha 14, 16, **16**
Benz, Eugen 14, 16
Benz, Karl 10, 12, 14, **14**, **16**, 19, 29
Benz, Karl (son) 16
Benz models
 16/50 sport 24
 Blitzen 21-22, **21-22**
 Comfortable 16
 Ideal 16, **17**
 Parsifal 21
 Patentmotorwagen 12, **13**, 15, **16**, 29, 36, 97
 three-wheeler **13**, 14, **15**
 Tropfenwagen 22
 Type 260 24
 Velociped (Velo) 16, 17
 Victoria 16, **16**
Blundell, Martin 116
Böhringer, Eugen 72, 73, 82, 87
Bracco, Giovanni 54
Bracq, Paul 71
Brauchitsch, M. von 39, 40
Breitschwerdt, Werner 82
Bruce-Brown, David 21
Bruderhaus Reutlingen 11
Burman, Bob 22

Caracciola, Rudi 40, 41, 51, 54
Clark, Jimmy 118
Corneillat, Marcel 47
Cugnot, Nicholas 9
Curtiss-Wright 64

Daimler
 logo 12
 Manufacturing Company, Long Island 19
 Maybach engine 10, **10**, **11**
 Motor Company Limited, Coventry 19
 Motoren Gesselschaft 12-13, 25
Daimler, Gottlieb 10, 12, 19, 25, 29
Daimler models
 2.0-supercharged 26

10/30 2.7-liter 25
16/40 4.0-liter 25
1901 racer 18
American 12
Krankenwagen 25
Moto Carriage 12
motorcycle **11**, 12, 97
Phoenix 18
Prince Heinrich 25
Quadricycle 12
Reitras **11**
Daimler, Paul 19, 24, 25
Daimler-Benz models
 Mannheim 28
 Silver Arrow 39
 Type 600 **27**, 28
 W25 39
Dennis, Ron 116
DePalma, Ralph 21
Donohue, Mark 80
Dugdale, John 46

Eaton,Robert, 126
Electronic Stability Program (ESP) 106-107, 122
Elskamp, Leon 25
Evans, Oliver 9

Fangio, Juan Manuel 32, 66
Fischer,Friedrich von 15
Fitch John 54
Fittipaldi, Emerson 118, 119
Ford, Henry 22
Ford Thunderbird 60
Formula I 114-115
Francis, Devon 68
Fraser, Ian 74
Frentzen, Henry-Harald 116
Frère, Paul 80

Ganss, Julius 15, 17
Geise, Carl 64
Gruppe, Erwin 54

Hakkina, Mika 116, 117
Harpel, Wilhelm 43, 47
Hearne, 21
Helfrich, Theo 54
Hémery, Victor 21
Hermann, Hans 81
Hill, James 8, 9
Hoffman, Max 60, 64
Hoppe, Otto 43
Hopper, Heinz C 64
Hubbert, Jürgen 95, 123
Hurley, Roy T 64
Huygens, Christian 9

Illien, Mario 114, 118

Jackson, Mike 106
Jellinek, Emil 18, **18**, 19, 21
Jellinek, Mercedes 18, **18**
Jenatzy, Camille 21
Jenkinson, Denis 54, 62
Jeffkins, Rupert 21

Kimas, Beverly Rae 43
Kissel, Wilhelm 26
Klenk, Hans 54
Kling, Karl 54, 81
Knight, Charles Y 24
Korff, Baron von 81
Kurrle, Herr 54
Kurz, Emma 11

Lang, Herman 40, 41, 54
Langen, Eugen 10
Langworth, Richard 22
Lamm, John/Michael 87, 95
Lehto, J.J. 114
Lenoir, Jean Joseph Etienne 9
Levassor, Emile 18
Levegh, Pierre 62
Lewandowski, Jürgen 26
Liebold, Hans 80
Ludvigsen, Karl 32,33,77,81,100
Lyons, William 19

Mahle, Eberhard 81
Mansell, Nigel 116
Maybach, Wilhelm 10, **10**, 11-12, 13, 18, 19, 124
Maybach
 Design Study 124-125
 Zeppelin 124
Mears, Rick 118
Melcher, Gerhard 105
Mercedes models
 10/40/65 two-seater 25
 130 38
 130V 39
 150 38
 160 38
 160V 38
 170/220 49
 170D 43
 170S 43
 170V 38, **38**, 43, 46
 180 47,49
 180 sedan 60
 180D 49
 190 series 89
 190 49, 104
 190C 49
 190E 89, 104
 190SEL 49, 102
 190SL **59**, 60, **60-61**, 68, **68-69**, 71, 72
 200 89

200 series 104
219 49
220 46, 47, 49
220 Cabriolet **42**, 43-45, **44**
220S 49-50, **50-51**
220S/SE Cabriolet **48**
220SE 50, **50-51**, 82
220SE sedan 81
230E 89
230SL **70-71**, 71, 72-73, **72**, 73-74, **74**, 82
230SL Roadster 72
230TE **90**
240D 91
240TD 90
250SE 82
250SL 73, **73**, 75
260E 89280C 101
280SEL4.5, 84
280SL 74-75, **75**, **76**, 77
280SLC 77
300 45-46, **45**, 46
300 sedan 56
300 series 49
300D 90
300E 89
300E2.6 89
300E24 89
300K 29
300S Coupe 53
300S Sports Coupe 52-53, **52**
300SE 82, 89
300SEL 82, 84, 89
300SEL3.5 84
300SEL6.3 82, 84
300SL 53-54, 55, 64, 72, 74, 76, 78, 92-93, 102
300SL-24 93
300SL Coupe 54, 56, **56**, **57**, **58**, 59-60, 62
300SL Roadster 54, 56, **58**, 59
300SLR 54, 62, 62-63, **62-63**
300TD
300TE **91**
330SL 68, 71
350SL 75, 76
350SL Coupe 75, 76
350SLC 79
370K 33
370K Mannheim 33
370S Mannheim 33
420SE 89
420SEL 89
450SL 76, **77**
450SLC 79, 77
500K 33, **34-35**
500SE **85**, 89
500SEL 89
500SL 93, 101
540K **37**, 64

540K Special Roadster 36
560SEL 89
560SL 77, **92**, **93**
600 89
600 Pullman **65**, 66, **66**, **67**, 68, 82
600 sedan 68
600SL 101
620Supercharged 29
630 29
630K **24**, 29, 30, **30**
680K 30
700SS 30
700SSK 31-32
720SSKL 31, **31**
770 Grosser Mercedes, 37
A140 121
A160 121
A170 121
C36 105
C43AMG 195
C111-I 78, **78**, 79, 100
C111-II **78-79**, 79-80
C111-III 80, **80**
C111-IV 80
C112 100, **100**
C180 104
C200 104
C220 104
C230 103
C280 101, 103, 105
CLK Cabriolet 109
CLK320 108
CLK320 Cabriolet 109
CLK320 Coupe 107-110, **107**, **108-109**
CLK430 Coupe 109
CLK-GT **84**
CLK-GTR racer **115**
E320 wagon 105, 106, **106**
ML320 47
ML320 **94**, **95**, **96**, **97**, **99**, **127**
R129 92,93
S320 111
S420 14
S500 111, **112-113**
S600 111, **111**
S650 111
SL280 93
SL Roadster 109
SLK Roadster 109
SLK230 101, **101**, **102**
SSK 66
W25 Racer 39-40, **39**
W120 47, 49
W123 89, 90
W124 89
W124 200 89
W125 40

W154 40-41, **40**
W165 51
W201 89, 104
W202 104

AAV 97
AMG racer 81
A-Class **120-121**, 121-123, **122**
All Activity Vehicle see AAV
American 19, **19**, 97
C-Class 88, **88**, **89**, 105, 107
C-Class sedan 47, **103**, 104, **104**
Compact see C-Class
Executive see E-Class
E-Class 105-106, 107
Gelandewagen see G-wagen
GP Mercedes 21
Grand Prix **20**, 21
Grey Ghost 21
Grosser 37-38 see also 600, 700
Gullwing Coupe see 300SL Coupe
G-wagen 87, **87**, 95
Kompaktklasse see C-Class
Mannheim 29
McLaren Mercedes **116**, **116-117**
M-Class 87, 95-97
Mittelerklasse see E-Class
Penske Mercedes **118**, **119**
Pontons 49-50
Sauber racer **82-83**, 100
S-Class 29, 105, 107, **110**, 111, **124**
S-Class sedan 47, 89
Silver Arrow 40, 50, 64, 117
Smart 123, **123**
Sonderklasse see S-Class
station wagons 90-91
Stuttgart 28, **28**, 29
Super see S-Class
Touristik and Transport see T series
T series 90-91
Type 630 **24**, 25
Micklin, Lance 62
Moch, Guido 80
Moll, Rolf 81
Morgan, Paul,114
Moss, Stirling 54, 59, 62, 66
Mueller, Oscar 19
Muller, Josef 71

Nallinger, Fritz 9, 12, 14, 26, 33, 43, 51, 71
Neubauer, Albert 40, 51
Nibel, Hans 21, 26, 29, 30, 31, 33, 38
Nedermeyer, Norbert 54
Niefer, Werner 114

Nitske, W. Robert 32
Norbye, Jim 68-69
Nuvolari, Tazio 39

Oldfield, Bernd Eli 22
Ott, Rolant 81
Otto, Nikolaus 9-10, **9**, 11, 12

Parktronic system 111
Penske, Roger 118
Porsche, Ferdinand 24, 25, **25**, 29, 30, 31, 47
Postlethwaite, Harvey 114

Renschler, Andreas 95, 96
Reiss, Fritz 54
Resta, Dario 21
Ringer, Bertha see Benz, Bertha
Ritter, August 14
Röhr, Gustav 36, 39
Rosqvist, Ewy 82

Sacco, Bruno 21, 39, 49, 56, 72, 92, 93, 100
Sailer, Max 36
Sazarin, Eduard 18
Sazarin, Madame 12, 18
Sauber, **82-83**, 100, 114
Schapiro, Jakob 26
Scherenberg, Hans 71
Schmidt, Heinz 79
Schock, Walter 81
Schrempp, Jürgen A. 123, 126
Schumaker, Michael 114, 116
Scott, David 68
Seaman, Dick 40
Simms, F.R. 19
SmartKey 109-110, **110**
Socher, Hermann 81
Socher, Hermann 81
Seinemann, Rico 80
Steiner, Kilian 12
Steinway William 19, **19**
Stern, Ritter von 21
Strauss, Dr Emil Georg von 26

Uhlenhaut, Rudolf 33, 40, 51, 79, 82
Unser, Al 118, 119

Wagner, Max 36
Wankel, Felix 79
Wendlinger, Karl 114, 116
Werner, Helmut 93, 102
Werner, Wilhelm 21
Wilfert,Karl 47, 54
Wilhelm II 37
Wirth, Ursula 82
Woelfert, 12
Wychodil, Arnold 64

PICTURE CREDITS: *David Gooley pp 2, 6, 24, 30, 34-36, 42-46, 48, 50-52, 55-61, 65-69, 73-77, 85, 88-89; Mercedes-Benz North America pp 2, 5, 9-11, 16, 18-19, 94-127; Mercedes-Benz Museum pp 2, 12-15, 17, 20-23, 25, 27-28, 31-33, 37-38, 40-41, 53-54, 62-64, 78-84, 91-93; Neill Bruce: Motoring Photolibrary pp 29, 39, 86; The Peter Roberts Collection c/o Neill Bruce: Motoring Photolibrary pp 70-72, 87, 90; John Heilig p 8.*

To a dear friend, & the best chauffeur we know! Happy 80th – January 30, 2002
Healthy Birthdays for years!

Love,
Phyllis
&
Richard